Red Books *showing the way*

COUNTY STREET ATLAS

NORTHAMPTONSHIRE

TOWN CENTRE STREET MAPS

Every effort has been made to verify the accuracy of information in this book but the publishers cannot accept responsibility for expense or loss caused by an error or omission.

Information that will be of assistance to the user of the maps will be welcomed.

Representation on these maps of a road, track or path is no evidence of the existence of a right of way.

Street plans prepared and published by
Red Books (Estate Publications) Ltd, Bridewell House, Tenterden, Kent, TN30 6EP.
Publishers acknowledge the co-operation of the local authorities of towns represented in this atlas.

Ordnance Survey®

This product includes mapping data licensed from Ordnance Survey® with the permission of the Controller of Her Majesty's Stationery Office.

Crown Copyright
Red Books (Estate Publications) Ltd
513-04/01-06
ISBN 1 84192 444 X
All rights reserved
Licence Number 100019031

www.redbooks-maps.co.uk

LEGEND

	Pedestrianized / Restricted Access
	Track
	Built Up Area
- - - -	Footpath
	Stream
	River
Lock	Canal
	Railway / Station
●	Post Office
P P+	Car Park / Park & Ride
C	Public Convenience
+	Place of Worship
→	One-way Street
i	Tourist Information Centre
▲8 ▲8	Adjoining Pages
	Area Depicting Enlarged Centre
	Emergency Services
	Industrial Buildings
	Leisure Buildings
	Education Buildings
	Hotels etc.
	Retail Buildings
	General Buildings
	Woodland
	Orchard
	Recreational / Parkland
	Cemetery

This **COUNTY STREET ATLAS** contains street maps for each town centre.
The street atlases listed below are **LOCAL STREET ATLASES**,
with comprehensive local coverage.

CORBY, KETTERING & WELLINGBOROUGH

including: Barton Seagrave, Broughton, Burrow's Bush, Burton Latimer, Cottingham, Desborough, Earls Barton, Finedon, Great Doddington, Hatton Park, Higham Ferrers, Irchester, Irthlingborough, Market Harborough, Raunds, Rothwell, Rushden, Stanion, Stanwick, Weldon, Wollaston etc.

MILTON KEYNES

including: Bletchley, Buckingham, Castlethorpe, Deanshanger, Fenny Stratford, Great Brickhill, Great Linford, Hanslope, Heath and Reach, Leighton Buzzard, Middleton, Newport Pagnell, Newton Longville, Shenley Wood, Stantonbury, Stoke Hammond, Two Mile Ash, Walton, Water Eaton, Woburn Sands, Wolverton, Yardley Gobion etc.

NORTHAMPTON

including: Boothville, Boughton, Brackmills, Bugbrooke, Collingtree, Dallington, Ecton, Great Houghton, Hardingstone, Hunsbury Hill, Kislingbury, Milton Malsor, Moulton, New Duston, Round Spinney, Spring Park, Weedon Bec, Weston Favell, Wootton etc.

RUGBY

including: Bilton, Brownsover, Cawston, Clifton upon Dunsmore, Crick, Dunchurch, Hillmorton, Kilsby, Long Lawford, Newbold on Avon, Overslade etc.

For a complete title listing please visit our website
www.redbooks-maps.co.uk

Scale of street plans: 4 Inches to 1 Mile (unless otherwise stated)

COUNTY STREET ATLASES

This atlas is intended for those requiring street maps of the historical and commercial centres of towns within the county. Each locality is normally presented on one or two pages and although, with many small towns, this space is sufficient to portray the whole urban area, the maps of large towns and cities are for centres only and are not intended to be comprehensive. Such coverage is offered in the Local Street Atlases (see Page 2).

County of Northamptonshire, estimated population 629,676

Districts: Boundaries of the districts are shown on pages 4-5.

District	Population	District	Population
Corby	53,174	Northampton	194,458
Daventry	71,838	South Northants	79,293
East Northants	76,550	Wellingborough	72,519
Kettering	81,844		

Population figures are based upon 2001 Census.

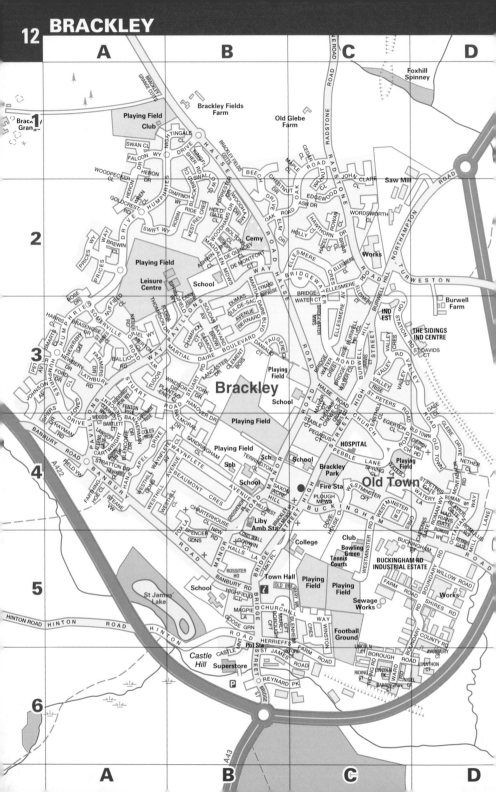

Burton Latimer

BURTON LATIMER BY-PASS

LATIMER PARK INDUSTRIAL ESTATE

KETTERING ROAD

WELLINGBOROUGH ROAD

Isham

River Ise

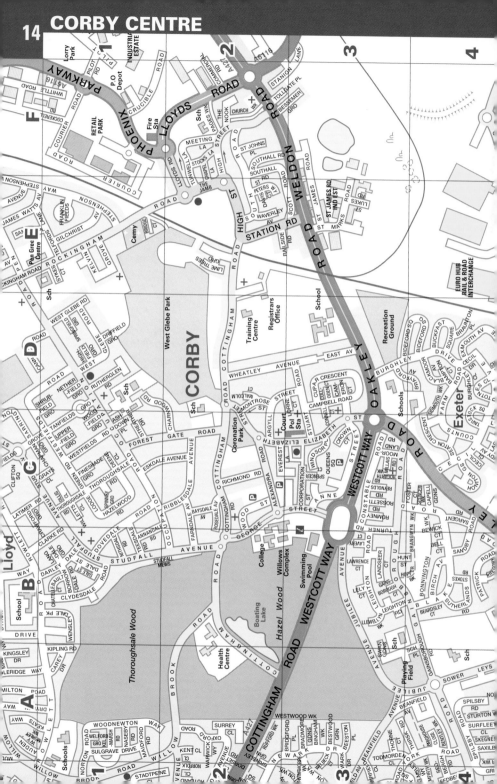

CRICK

A B C D

1

Factory

Hotel

M1
JUNCTION 18
A428

MAIN
ROAD CRICK BY - PASS

Grand Union Canal

Crick
Wharf

ELDON
WAY

ELDON

M1

2

ELDON
CL

INDUSTRIAL ESTATE

WAY MAIN

Playing
Field

BARLEY
CFT
EVERTOFT
DRAYSON
LA
OAK LA
CHURCH LANE
PORTLOW
ELLEN
STYLE CLOSE
KING
BUCKWELL'S
RECTORY CLOSE STREET
Hall
Sewage
Works

School

DUNN
COLEMAN
FALLOWFIELDS
PIKE
THORNTON
ASHWORTH
CL
BURY
DYKE
MONKS WY
MORSEL

Crick

ROAD

Crick
Wharf

CHAPEL LA
THE PADDOCK
HIGH STREET
THE DERRY
MARSH
CL
THE MARSH
LAUDS ROAD
SOUTHFIELDS
DR
BOAT HORSE LA

3

MARSONS
DR
WELL
HL CL
ASHBY DR
THE
HIGH LEYS
WATFORD
ROAD

Crick
Tunnel

DEANSHANGER

Comm
Centre

Play
Area

DEANSHANGER ROAD

4

GLEBE ROAD
HIGH
VIEW
GLEBE
VIEW
HIGH
PUXLEY
RIDGMONT
VIEW
NORTH
WY
WINWOOD
CL
PUXLEY ROAD
HAYES
PUXLEY ROAD

Shrob
Spinney

Chantry
Farm

ROAD

AVENUE
RIDGMONT
CL
NORTH
WAY
THISTLE
DSNELL
CL
HONEY HILL DR

Deanshanger

WESTFIELD
ELM DR
ELM
DRIVE
RIDGMONT
THE
RIDINGS
RIDGMONT
ROAD
PORTER'S CL
DISNELL
WY
NERIS
BROOK
GRASMERE
FOXHOLES CL
HAYES

5

Liby

ROAD
LITTLE LONDON
SPRINGFIELD
BDSW
ELL
GDNS
ROBERT
CL
SHARMANS
Scout
Hall

HIGH
STREET

HAYES RD

Northfields
Buckingham Arm

PASSENHAM LANE

Manor
Farm

Playing
Field

BROOK WAY
CHURCH LA
THE GREEN
DOVE
CFT
BEECHER
Primary
School
PATRIDGE
STRATFORD
BUCKINGHAM ROAD
Canal

Foot
Bridge

Kingsbrook
School

Tennis
Courts

Playing
Field

ROAD

Pit

6

Ma
Ho

Playing
Fields

A422

A B C D

nall

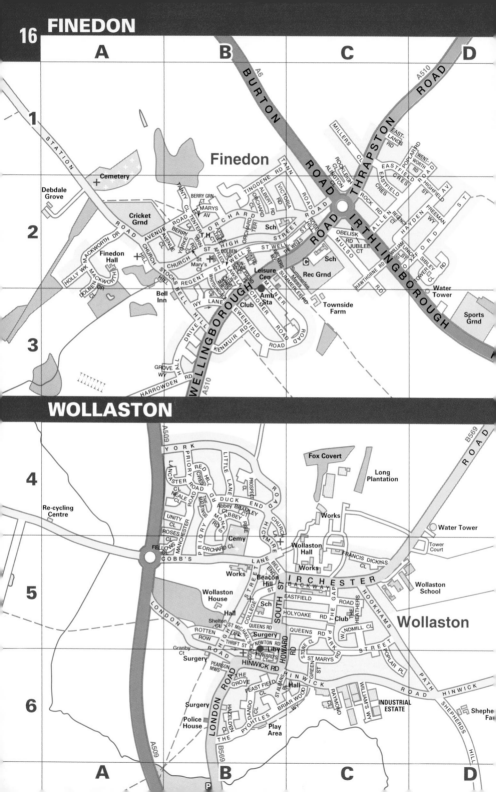

A B C D

1
2
3

Finedon

STATION
Cemetery
Debdale Grove
Cricket Grnd
Finedon Hall
MACKWORTH DR
HOLLY WK
MACKWORTH
DOLBEN CL
CHURCH
STOCKS HILL
BELL
AVENUE
ROAD
BERRY
VANITY CT
CEMETERY
BERRY GRN CT
ST MARYS AV
TINGDENE RD
ALBERT RD
ORCHARD RD
VICTORIA RD
TANN ROAD
HIGH ST
ST
Mary's Cl
REGENT ST
IVY LANE
DRIVE
HILL
HALL
GROVE WY
KENMUIR RD
EWENFIELD ROAD
HARROWDEN RD
WELLINGBOROUGH
A510
DOLBEN CL
WHITBURN ST
MILL LANE
ST WELL ST
ST WELL ST
SUMMERLEE RD
CROWER
Leisure Cen
Club
Amen Sta
Sch
ST
WELLS RD
THE WELLS
MULSO
OBELISK RD
JUBILEE CT
BURTON ROAD
A6
THRAPSTON ROAD
IRTHLINGBOROUGH
ROAD
MILLERS
ROCKINGM
CLINGTON RD
ALINGTON RD
ROCK RD
ALLEN RD
HAWTHORNE RD
C
Sch
Rec Grnd
Townside Farm
Water Tower
Sports Grnd
EAST-LANDS RD
A510 ROAD
EASTFIELD CRES
EASTFIELD CRES
HAYDEN RD
POPPLAR RD
WENT-WORTH
HIGHFIELD RD
SIBLEY RD
FREEMAN WY
UNION ST
WILLIAM RD
TOWER RD
OXFORD ST

4
5
6

Wollaston

Re-cycling Centre
A509 ROAD
YORK RD
PRIORY ROAD
LANCASTER CL
NEALE CL
UNITY CL
ROSES CL
MANCHESTER
ORCHARD CL
FELTONS
COBB'S
LITTLE LANE
RED HILL CREST
ABBEY
BRAMLEY RD
THE MALTINGS
ABBEY RD
Cemy
DUCK END
PROSPECT RD
CHURCH RD
HICKMIRE
Fox Covert
Long Plantation
Works
Works
Wollaston Hall
FRANCIS DICKINS
IRCHESTER
BACKWAY
Beacon Hill
Wollaston House
Hall
Shelton Ct
ST MICHAEL
Granby Ct
Surgery
LONDON ROAD
COLLEGE STREET
BELL LANE
SOUTH ST
Sch
EASTFIELD
HOLYOAKE RD
QUEENS RD
THRIFT ST
NEWTON RD
HINWICK RD
Liby
HOWARDS
PEARSON MWS
ROTTEN ROW
THE GROVE
FEAST FIELD
HAZELDON
BRIAR WOOD WY
PYGTLES
DANDO CL
PLAY Area
Police House
THE B569
Surgery
QUEENS RD
ST MARYS
GREEN END
HINWICK
THE GARDENS
THE HEATHERS
PARK RD
WNDMILL CL
Club
Works
WILLIAM'S WY
RAYMOND
INDUSTRIAL ESTATE
POPLAR PL
HOOKHAMS PATH
ROAD
STREET
HINWICK
SHEPHERDS HILL
Water Tower
Tower Court
Wollaston School
B569 ROAD
RD

A B C D

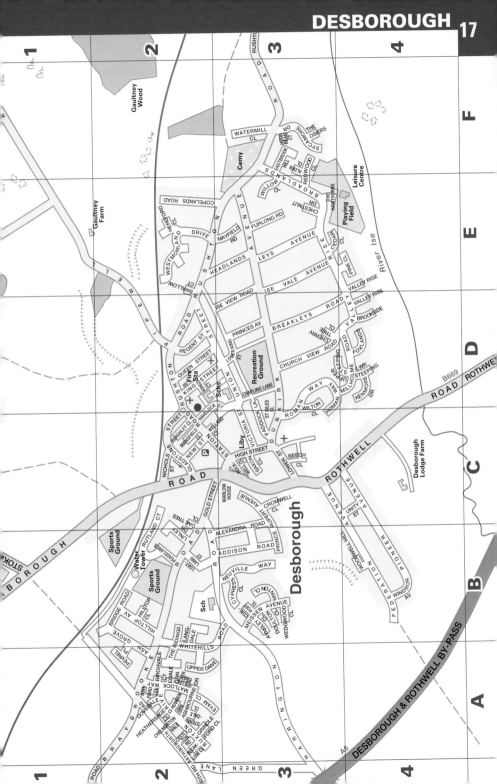

Gaultney Wood

Gaultney Farm

WATERMILL CL

Cemy

WATTON

THE OSIERS

SYCAMORE

EASTBROOK

BEAM HILL

REDWOOD CL

BROADPLAT

THE HAWTHORNS

Leisure Centre

Playing Field

COPELANDS ROAD

HEREFORD CL

WESTMORLAND

SWALLOW CT

DRIVE

MAYFIELD RD

FURLONG RD

AVENUE

CHESTNUT

CEDAR CL

PINE CL

HEADLANDS

LEYS

AVENUE

ISE VIEW ROAD

ISE VALE AVENUE

River Ise

REGENT STREET

QUEEN STREET

UNION STREET

PRINCES AV

BREAKLEYS ROAD

VALLEY RISE

VALLEY RISE

BROOKSIDE

CHERRY TREE CL

FOYLANDS

RUSHTON ROAD

Fire Sta

Schs

LOWER KING

CHAPLINS LANE

Recreation Ground

CHURCH VIEW ROAD

SPEEDING ROAD

MILL HOLME

LWR STEEPING

KENMORE DR

B669

ROAD ROTHWELL

Desborough Lodge Farm

KIRK

PADDOCK LA

ST GILES ST

VICTORIA ST

ROMAN WAY

ROMAN WILTON CL

BIRTLEY CL

MANSFIELD RD

HAVELOCK RD

NEW ST

WELLAND

HIGH STREET

SAXON ST

BEECH CL

Liby

WELL LA

LOWER ST

NICHOLS ST

GLADSTONE ST

GOLD STREET

MARLOW HOUSE

CROMWELL

ROAD

RUTLAND CT

OAK TREE

LINLEY CT

PENSERDANS

ALEXANDRA

PRINCE

ROAD

ROAD

Desborough

ROAD

ROTHWELL

FEDERATION AVENUE

PIONEER

UNITY ST

WOODHILL

WINDSOR AV

Sports Ground

Water Tower

Sports Ground

Sch

BRIDGE ROAD

HILLTOP CL

ASH GROVE

FEVREL PL

WHITEHILLS

THE RIDINGS

LANGDALE

BIRCHVALE

UPPER DANE

ROAD

LAND ST

ADDISON

NEVILLE WAY

CYPRESS CL

DOLTON CL

WEDGWOOD CL

AINSLEY AVE

MESSEN AVE

HARRINGTON ROAD

KEMPTON

BLAM

MATLOCK WAY

EDALE

ROOKE WAY

ASHBOURNE DR

EYAM CL

GRINDLE

FORD CL

COVERDALE

HEATHERSIDE

DALE

BRAY

GREEN LANE

STOKE

BOROUGH

DESBOROUGH & ROTHWELL BY-PASS

A5

ROAD

A   B   C   D

1

MAIN ROAD

Main Road Farm

A4500

WELLINGBOROUGH

Cemy

WHITE HOUSE INDUSTRIAL ESTATE

MEARS ASHBY RD

MAIN

B573

NORTHAMPTON

Playing Field

The Grange

New Lodge

Pol Sta

AVENUE

TITLEY BAWK AV

INDUSTRIAL ESTATE

MALLARD

BARON

CLOSE

ROAD

Grange Farm

Water Tower

New Barton

2

ELIZABETH

TOWNLEY WY

STREETON

GRANGE CL

MANOR

Amb Sta

WHITE WY

MANOR

BERRY

HORNBY RD

THE PYGHTLE

BROOKES MEWS

KING

ELIZABETH VICTORIA

NORTH ST

STREET

VICTORIA

VICTORIA CL

WELLINGBOROUGH RD

PRINCE

QUEEN ST

ST

ST

STEVENS CT

WEST WY

HARROWICK LA

DR S471

ROAD

Rec Grnd

Youth Club

WILLIAM ST

KNIGHTS CT

HORTH

MANOR RD

NESBITT'S YD

BORDERS

THE DELL

Fire Sta

ROAD

SPENCER CL

MILLS CL

CHURCHILL

CLARKE

ST CRISPIN RD

WOODLANDS GRANGE

Depot

3

WEST

STREET

CAMPBELL SQ

PARK CL

PARK LA

SUNNY SIDE

ST

LONDON END

THE SQ

BROAD

HIGH STREET

Hall

Mus

Schs

FAIRHURST

Liby

DODDINGTON

ROAD

NEW ST

SPRING

CORDON CRES

COWPER CL

GRAY CL

BURNS CL

KEATS CL

CLARE CL

DODDINGTON

MILL

Depot

Factory

STATION

HARCOURT SQ

Harcourt Mews

Bowling Grn & Tennis Cts

Works

AGGATE

WAY

GRENDON

A45

ROAD

STATION

SAXON RISE

WILSON WAY

DOWTHORPE END

BARKER WY

SHEFIELD RD

ALLEBONE RD

COMPTON

THORPE RD

COMPTON WAY

ROAD

MOUNT PLEASANT

SHURVILLE CL

GARDENS

MILBURY

CORDON CRES

OXFORD CL

BALMORAL

BURNS CL

KEATS CL

CLARE CL

Mill Lane Farm

Earls Barton

The Millbarn Cottage

LANE

Mill House

4

5

Weir

Concrete Recycling Centre

GRENDON

ROAD

River Nene

Depot

Sports Ground

River Nene

6

A   B   Lock   C   D

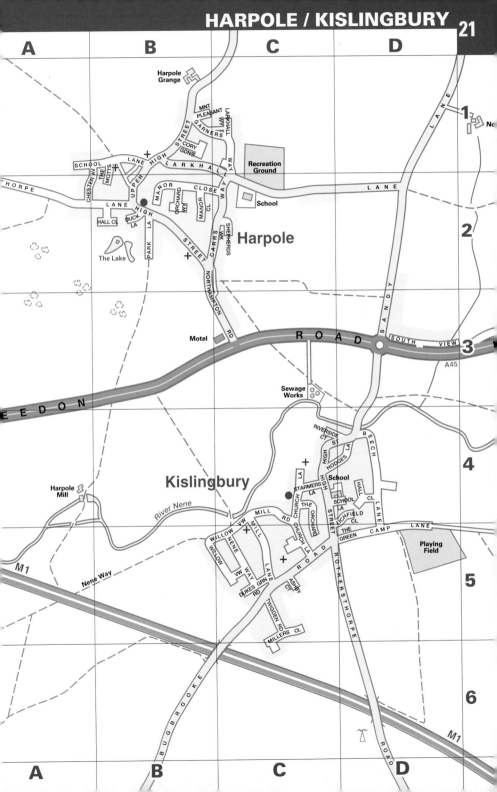

Harpole

Kislingbury

Harpole Grange

MNT PLEASANT WY
LARKHALL WY
GARNERS
HIGH STREET
CORY GDNS
LARKHALL
SCHOOL
THE MOTTS
CHESTER AV
UPPER HIGH LANE
MANOR WY
ORCHARD WY
MANOR CL
CLOSE
SHEPHERDS WK
CARRS
HALL CL
DUCK LA
HIGH STREET
PARK LA
NORTHAMPTON RD

The Lake

Recreation Ground

School

School

LANE

1
2
3
4
5
6

No

LANE

SANDY

Motel

R O A D

SOUTH VIEW

A45

E E D O N

Sewage Works

RIVERSIDE CT
HIGH ST
HODGES LA
BEECH LANE
STARMERS LA
HALL CL
SCHOOL
LICHFIELD CL
THE ORCHARD
CHURCH LA
CHURCH RD
HIGH STREET
ROTHERSTHORPE
THE GREEN
CAMP LANE
MILL RD
WILLOW VW
WILLOW WAY
NENE WAY
DUKES GRN RD
ASHBY CT
TWIGDEN RD
MILLERS CL

School

Harpole Mill

River Nene

M 1

Nene Way

Playing Field

M 1

B U G B R O O K E

R O A D

A **B** **C** **D**

1

2

3

4

5

6

Freestones Farm

Playing Field

RUGBY DR

GARDEN FIELDS

LANGLEY CRES

FETTLEDINE AV

CHURCHILL AV

WELFORD

THE SHORTLANDS

CLARKE CL

PALMER

Cor

Frontier Lodge

Adv

Knightlands

NOBLE AVENUE

ALEXANDER RD

ALEXANDER PL

Pol Sta

Crow Hill

A6

SCOTS MERE

Factory

WYCKLEY

HOLBUSH WY

LONG ACRES

MIDDLE GRASS

MEREFIELDS

TURNBROOK CL

FITZWILLIAM

Knightlands

The Farm

By Pass Farm

Diamonds Business Centre

ATTLEY WAY

MARSH LANE

Football Pitches

FINEDON

B5348

RINDWELL

GARROW

GATES CL

HOLBUSH

SCHARPWELL

DRAYTON

MOUNTFIELD RD

PORTLAND

DRAYTON

DRAYTON PL

SPRING

SPRING

BROOK TER

ARCHFIELD TER

ROAD

ADDINGTON RD

ROAD

A6

Huxlow School

FERNMOOR DR

HIGHFIELD RD

LILLEY

SPRING ST

NEW ST

EAST TER

LOVELL

Manor Mews

Works

Depot

Rushden & Diamonds Football Grnd

Factory

STATION

STATION ROAD

Central Recreation Ground

NURSERY

SONS

SCHS

Civic Hall

Schs

Market Cross

ST

CHURCH ST

NENE

MEETING LA

MELL

MANOR DR

Liby

Weir

Sports Ground

SCARBOROUGH CL

MANTON RD

EXCELSIOR

COLL

Hall

CP

The Homes

Louisa Lilley

OAK TER

ST PETERS

VW

SONS

LINE

TER

MANOR CT

Car S

QUEEN ST

MUSSON CL

STREET

Surgery

SPINNEY CL

NENE

WATERS

Cricket Ground

JUBILEE

Hargrave ST

LEES ST

Works

Liby

Med Cen

PARK ROAD

THE CLOSE

Cemy

MEADOW WY

GREENFIELD

Irthlingborough

Club

WINDMILL LA

Amb Sta

Hall

BAKER

STANSON

WILSON CRES

CHERRY

GEORGE ST

VICTORIA RD

WATES

Pol Ho

SPENCER RD

NICHOLAS LA

CROUCH RD

NENE WY

River Nene

River Nene Navigation

Nursing Home

ALLEN RD

WELLINGBOROUGH ROAD

B571

COWPER WK

CLAXTON

MARKET

VALE

CHERRY ST

A

JOHN PYEL RD

NICHOLAS RD

TANNERY COTTS

River Nene

CHOWNS MILL BUSINESS PARK

BRIGHTWELL WK

FLAXWK

GREEN

LAWWOOD

BYPASS

WILLIAM

PERKINS CL

PREMIER CL

DRY WK

WHITWORTH RD

TRIGG CL

BRAWN CL

Weir

RAVENSFORD WK

SWOW

DIAMOND

LUCAS RD

VALE

Nene

THE SIDINGS

WAT CL

EBB WY

DAIRY RD

HOME CL

FLOOD WY

RYEHILL CL

ULLSWATER

CONISTON

WINDERMERE WY

GRASMERE

LAKESIDE

A **B** **C** **D**

32

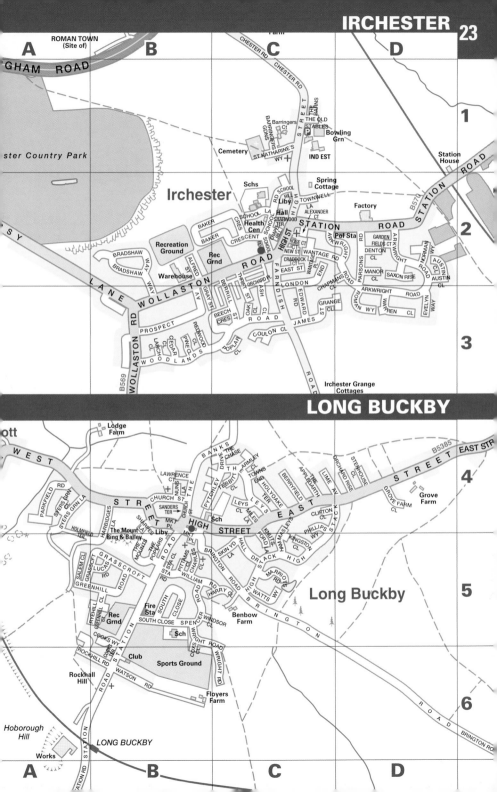

IRCHESTER

A | B | C | D

ROMAN TOWN
(Site of)

'GHAM ROAD

Farm

CHESTER RD

CHESTER RD

1

THE PLAINS
THE OLD
STABLES

Station
House

ster Country Park

Barringers
Ct

BARRINGERS
GDNS

St STREET

Cemetery

ST. KATHARINE'S
WY

Bowling
Grn

IND EST

B570 STATION ROAD

Irchester

Schs

Spring
Cottage

Factory

2

Schs
RD SCHOOL
Liby
HILL

SCHOOL
CRES

Hall
SHARWOOD
TER
HIGH ST
Health
Cen
ROSE CT
NEW ST
CRESCENT
CRADDOCK
EAST ST
FARNDISH

TOWNWELL
LA
ALEXANDER
CT

STATION ROAD

ARKWRIGHT RD

Pol Sta

GARDEN
FIELDS CT
DENTON
CL

MANOR
CL

SAXON RISE

ARKWRIGHT ROAD

NORMAN RD

AUSTIN RD

AUSTIN CL

Recreation
Ground

BRADSHAW
WAY

BRADSHAW
WAY

ALFRED RD

GRAY ST

Rec
Grnd

BAKER CRES

BAKER CRES

Warehouse

BERRILL ST

ORCHARD PL

THRIFT ST

ASH RD

WANTAGE RD
WANTAGE RD

LONDON END

EDWARD RD

JAMES

CHAPMANS RD

GRANGE RD

WREN CL

RENN WY

PARSONS RD

EVELYN WAY

WOLLASTON

WOLLASTON RD

B569

PROSPECT

REDWOOD CL

CEDAR CL

LARCH CL

PINE CL

BEECH CRES

OAK RD

POPLAR

COULON CL

3

WOODLANDS

Irchester Grange
Cottages

LONG BUCKBY

ott

Lodge
Farm

WEST

B5385 EAST STR

STREET

4

Parkfield
RD

SYERS GRN

SYERS GRN LA

HOLMFIELD TER

HARBIDGES LA

LAWRENCE
CT

NUNS LA

CHURCH ST

SANDERS
TER

MKT PL

CHURCH ST

SHARPES LA

BANKS

DRIVE

THE CHASE

THE
TH

PYTCHLEY

TEBBITT

ARMLEY

TOWNS
END

BERRYFIELD

HOLYOAKE
TER

APPLEHEARTH

THE LIME

EAST

LIME AV

ORCHARD RISE

STENHOUSE
CL

STREET

GROVE FARM
CL

Grove
Farm

The Mount
Ring & Bailey

Liby

HIGH

The POPLARS

LUCAS RD

SALEM CL

GRASSCROFT RD

GREENHILL CL

GREENHILL

PYEHILL CL

Rec
Grnd

COOKS WY

ROCKHILL RD

The MOUNTS

THE MOUNTS

Sch

LEYS CL

LEYS

MILES

MKT PL

STREET

SKIN YD

CLIFTON CL

HALL LA

KNUTSFORD LA

PITTAMS RD

BRINGTON RD

WILLIAM RD

RORY CL

HARRY CL

SOUTH CLOSE

SPENCER

WINDSOR

WRIGHT RD

WRIGHT ROAD

DRACK CL

WATTS

MARRIOTT RD

KINGSTON WY

PHILLIPS

HIGH

Long Buckby

5

Fire
Sta

SOUTH
CLOSE

STATION RD

Sch

Benbow
Farm

BRINGTON

Rockhall
Hill

STATION RD

Club

WATSON RD

Sports Ground

FLOYERS FARM RD

Floyers
Farm

6

Hoborough
Hill

Works

LONG BUCKBY

ROAD

BRINGTON RD

A | B | C | D

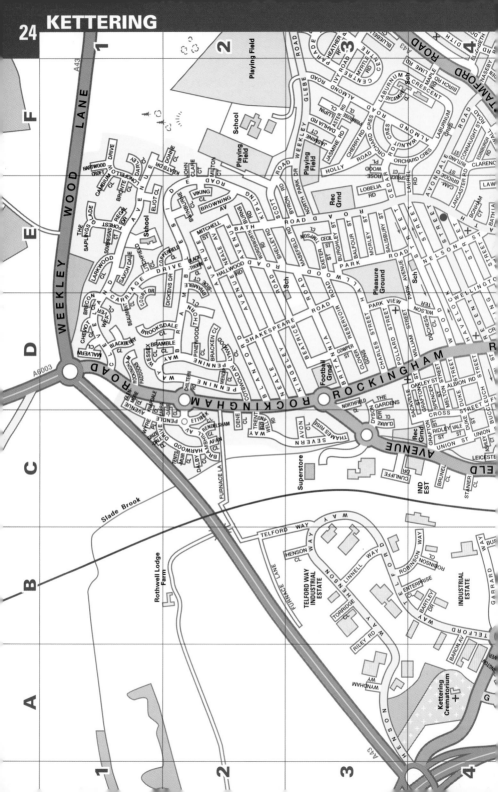

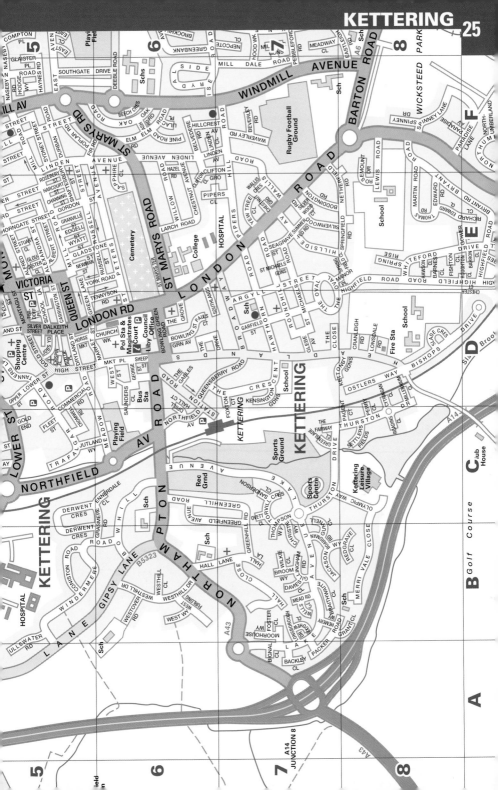

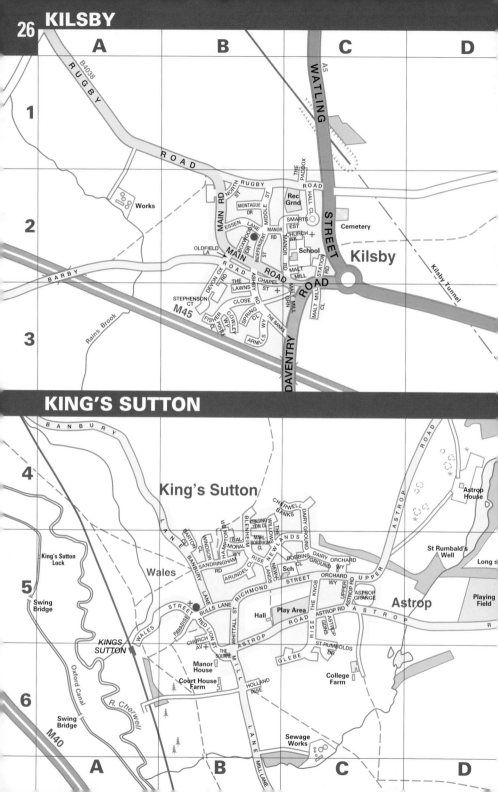

KILSBY

A B C D

1

B4038

RUGBY

WATLING

A5

ROAD

Works

MAIN RD

NORTH ST

MIDDLE ST

RUGBY ST

THE PADDOX

ROAD

HALL CL

Rec Grnd

MONTAGUE DR

ESSEX LANE

MANOR RD

SMARTS EST

CHURCH WK

STREET

Cemetery

2

Kilsby

BARBY

OLDFIELD LA

MAIN ROAD

BOXWOOD DR

INDEPENDENT ST

MANOR RD

School

MALT MILL

STATION RD

Kilsby Tunnel

DEVON OX RD

CHAPEL ROAD

THE LAWNS

ASHBY ST

MALT MILL GRN

MALT MILL CL

M45

STEPHENSON CT

CLOSE

COWLEY WY

FISHER RD

SPRING CL

THE BANKS

THISTLE WY

ARM'LS WY

3

Rains Brook

DAVENTRY ROAD

KING'S SUTTON

A B C D

BANBURY

ROAD

4

King's Sutton

LANE

BARTON LANE

CHERWELL BANKS

DAIRY GROUND

ASTROP

Astrop House

WINDSOR CL

HAMPTON RD

BLENHEIM

KENSING-TON CL

WILLOW CL

BAL-MORAL WY

MARL BOROUGH CL

THE NEWLANDS

DOBBINS CL

DAIRY GROUND

ORCHARD WY

St Rumbald's Well

Long S

King's Sutton Lock

Wales

SANDRINGHAM RD

ARUNDEL CL

RISE

NEWF'LANDS

ORCHARD STREET

Sch

UPPER ASTROP RD

UPPER ASTROP RD

ASTROP GRANGE

Astrop

Playing Field

5

Swing Bridge

BANBURY LANE

BULLS LANE

RICHMOND

WHITTALL ST

Hall

Play Area

RISE THE KNOB

ASTROP RD

ASTROP GDNS

R

WALES STREET

PARADISE STREET

RED LION ST

ASTROP ROAD

ROAD

ST RUMBOLDS DR

KINGS SUTTON

CHURCH AV

THE SQUARE

MILL LANE

GLEBE

6

Oxford Canal

Swing Bridge

R. Cherwell

Manor House

Court House Farm

HOLLAND RISE

College Farm

M40

Sewage Works

A B C D

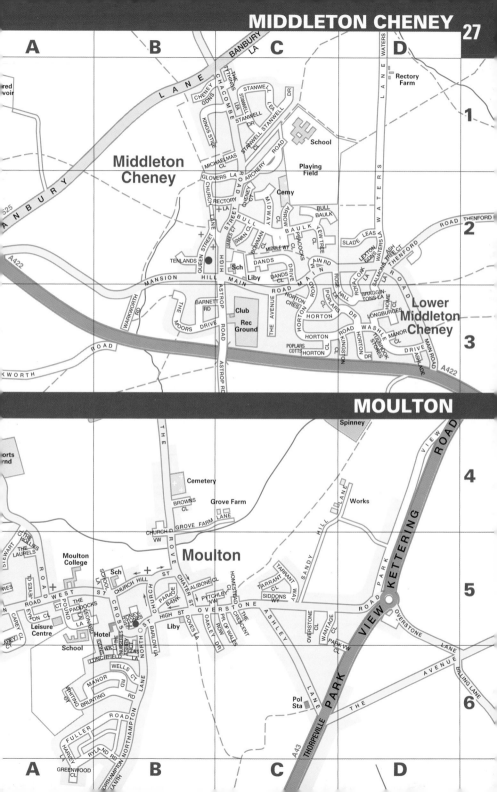

A **B** **C** **D**

BANBURY LA

WATERS LANE

Rectory Farm

red voir

CHACOMBE

CHEENEY GDNS

THE TITHINGS

KINGS STILE

STANWELL CL

STANWELL DR

STANWELL STANWELL

STANWELL DR

ROAD

ARCHERY

1

School

Playing Field

Middleton Cheney

MICHAELMAS CL

GLOVERS LA

CHURCH LANE

CHEENEY RD

RECTORY LA

MIDWAY

Cemy

BULL BAULK

THENFORD ROAD

2

BANBURY LANE

A422

JAMES STREET

BULL

SWAN CL

ROWNAN

MIDDLE WY

BAULK

ARROW

PEACOCK'S

YEW TREE

SLADE

LEAS

LEXTON GDNS

WATERS LA

THENFORD

SALMONS STREET

TENLANDS

QUEEN STREET

HIGH

Sch

Liby

DANDS

DANDS CL

MAIN RD

ROSE HILL

ROYAL OAK

HOME

BRAGGIN-TONS LA

LONGBURGES

Lower Middleton Cheney

MANSION HILL

MAIN

ASTROP ROAD

DRIVE

THE MOORS DRIVE

BARNETT RD

WARWORTH RD

Club Rec Ground

THE AVENUE

ROAD

HORTON CRES

POPLARS

HORTON

HORTON

POPLARS DR

KINGSTON ROAD

WASHBROOK STONES

HORTON DR

MANOR CL

MAIN ROAD

ASHLADE DRIVE

A422

3

WARWORTH

ROAD

POPLARS COTTS

HORTON

THE

Spinney

VIEW ROAD

4

orts rnd

Cemetery

BROWNS CL

Grove Farm

GROVE FARM LANE

LANE

SANDY HILL

Works

KETTERING

CHURCH VW

Moulton

GROVE

Moulton College

Sch

SCHOOL ST

LA

CHATER ST

ST

ALIBONE CL

PITCHLEY WY

TARRANT WY

TARRANT WY

SIDDONS WY

HOMESTEAD RD

PR OF WALES

ASHLEY

THE CRESCENT

PARK VW

OVERSTONE CL

WANTAGE CL

PARK

VIEW

Overstone

OVERSTONE LANE

5

STEWART

CT

THE HOLLIES

THE LAURELS

JESSOP

ROAD

WK

CL

EYTON

WEST

CAREY LA

THE PADDOCKS

LEONARD

POUND LA

CHURCH HILL

CHURCH ST

BANK

PARADE

HIGH ST

OAKLEY DR

DOVES LA

OVERSTONE RD

BILLING LANE

ABBEY CL

Leisure Centre

School

Hotel

HONEY STONES

Liby

CROSS ST

BARLOW LA

NORTH LANE

NURSERIES

THE GDNS

AVENUE

6

MANOR CL

WELLS CT

RD

LINCHFIELD

WHITING CT

BRUNTING

ROAD

Pol Sta

THORPEVILLE LANE

PARK VIEW

THE

FULLER

HARVEY

RYLAND RD

GREENWOOD CL

NORTHAMPTON

A43

A **B** **C** **D**

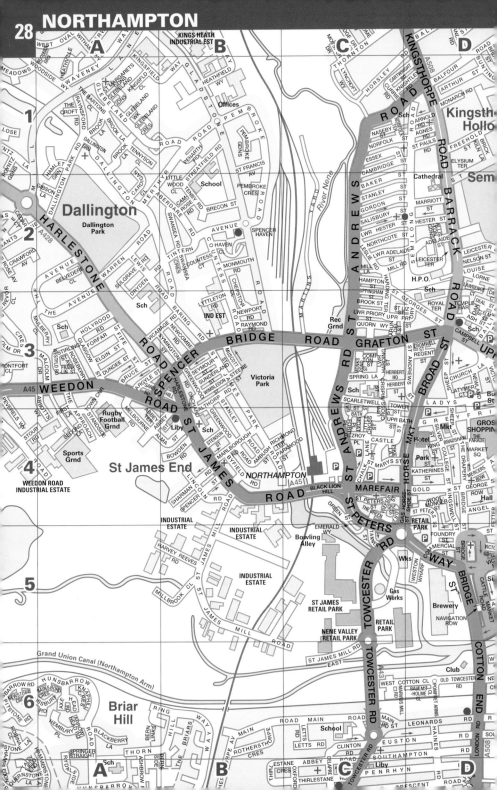

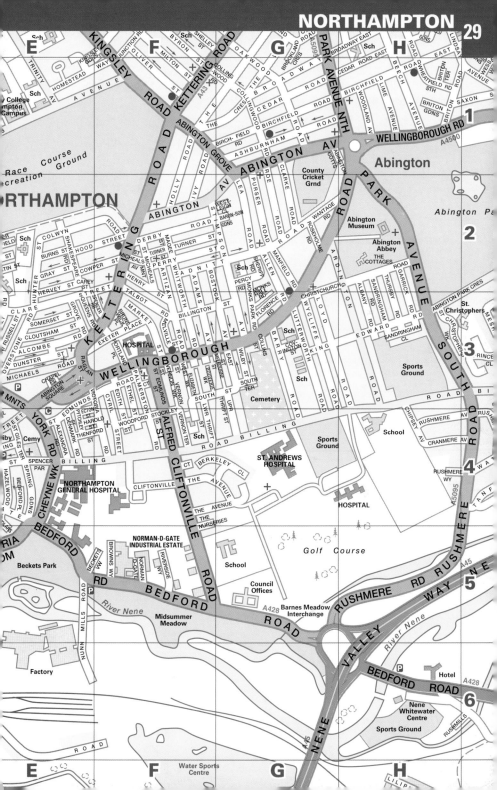

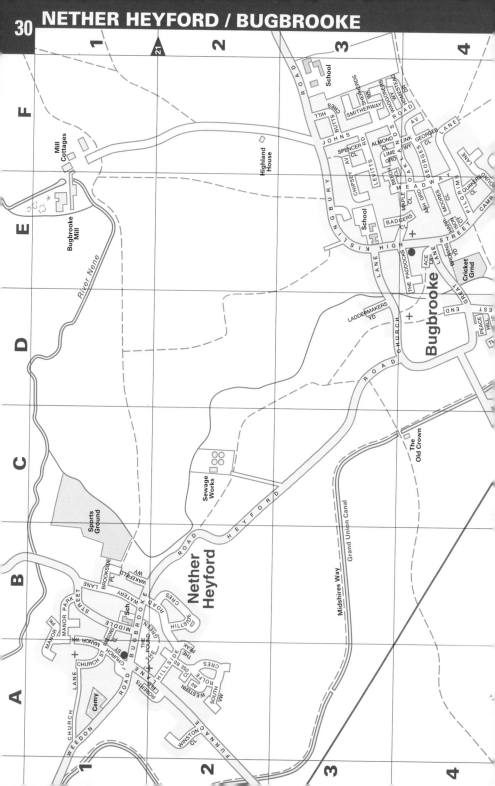

NETHER HEYFORD

Bugbrooke

Bugbrooke Mill

Mill Cottages

Highland House

River Nene

Sports Ground

Sewage Works

School

Cricket Grnd

The Old Crown

Grand Union Canal

Midshires Way

ROAD

HEYFORD ROAD

CHURCH ROAD

KISLINGBURY LANE

HIGH ST

CHURCH ROAD

LADDERMAKERS YD

THE PADDOCKS

GREAT ST

PEACE HILL

SHEPHERDS WK

WAGGONERS

SMITHERWAY

HILL BUTTS

JOHNS

SPENCER AV

CHIPSEY AV

CL

LEVITTS

ALMOND CL

LIME GRO

BEECH CL

MEADOW WY

MAPLE CL

ASH GRO

HARR MOORES

GEORGES CL

QUAKER CL

PILGRIMS CL

BROWNS YD

BADGERS CL

WINSTON RD

FURNACE LANE

WEEDON ROAD

CHURCH LANE

MANOR PK

MANOR WK

MIDDLE ST

BROOKSIDE PL

WAKEFIELD WY

BUGBROOKE ROAD

THE GREEN

WATERY LANE

HILLSIDE RD

ROLFE CRES

WESTERN AV

SOUTH VW

THE PEAK

HILLS RD

ROBERTS

Cem'y

Sch

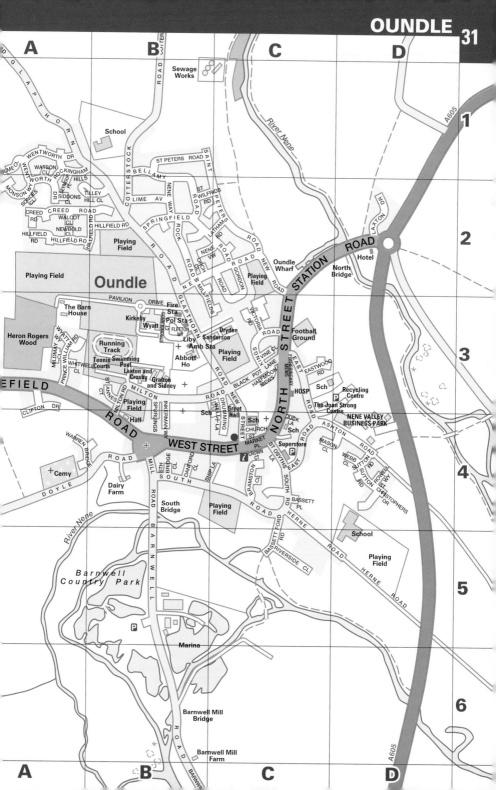

Higham Ferrers

Warmonds Hill

The Ferrers School

Midland Business Centre

INDUSTRIAL ESTATE

Rec Grnd

Recreation Ground

Chichele Coll

Almshouses

College

Works

Nene Valley Farm

Club

Bowling Green

The Moors

Sewage Works

Weir

Ski Slopes

Needle & Awl P.H.

Superstore

CROWN

River Nene

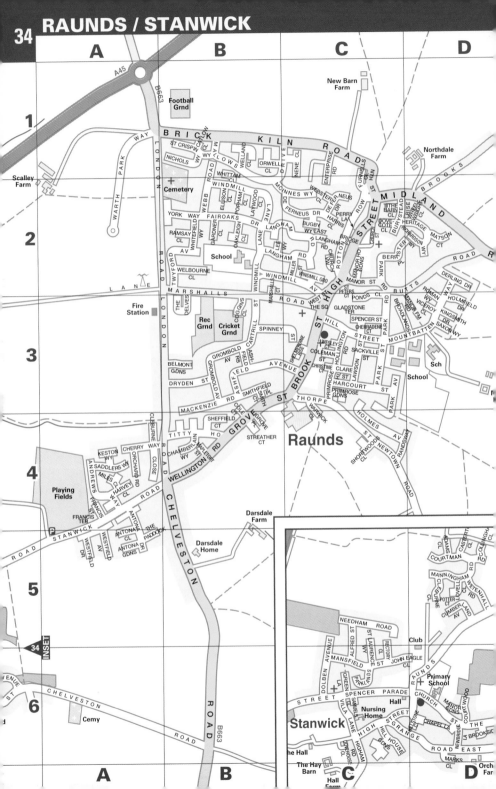

A   B   C   D

1
2
3
4
5
6

A45

B663

New Barn Farm

Football Grnd

Northdale Farm

Scalley Farm

BRICK KILN ROAD

MIDLAND ROAD

ST CRISPIN WY
NICHOLS CL

Cemetery

WHITTAM CL

WINDMILL LANE

ORWELL CL
NENE CL
ENTERPRISE CL

WEBSTER CL
NEUS CL
PERRY LA
HARRIS CL
BRIDGE

WELLAND
McINNES WY
DE FERNEUS DR
RICHARDSON WY
HERITAGE
MATSON CT

TITHE BARN CL
DOVE COTE CL
BURY STEAD

YORK WAY
FAIROAKS
RAMSAY CL
WELBOURNE CL

WEBB
WHITEFIELD WY
GARDNER WY
OAKLEIGH DR
TOPHAM CL
ELLISON DR
LAYWOOD DR

LANGHAM LANE
LANGHAM WY
LANGHAM RD

BUGBY WY EAST

LANGHAM ST

School

DERLING DR
HOLMFIELD CL
KINGSMITH
SAXON WY
ROMAN WY
VICEROY

HIGH STREET
ROTTON ROW
FURNELL

MANOR RD
CHURCH ST
BERR PL
MANOR ST
PARK RD

ROAD

WARTH PARK WAY
LONDON ROAD

LANE

MARSHALLS
THE DELVES
WEST ST
WINDMILL ST
MARSHALL ST
WINDMILL AV
WINDMILL GRO

Fire Station

Rec Grnd
Cricket Grnd

SPINNEY
CARTRILL ST
COGGINS RD
GROMBOLD AV
ASHFIELD RD
SMITHFIELD
CRISP PL
AVENUE

BROOK ST
GROVE ST
HILL

THE SQ
GLADSTONE TER
PONDS
SPENCER ST
CHERRADENE CT
WESLEYAN
COLEMAN ST
CHRISTINE CL
PRIMROSE
STREET
HOLLINGTON RD
SACKVILLE
CLARE ST
LAWSON ST
HARCOURT
PRIMROSE GDNS

BUTTS
BROADLANDS
PARK RD
MOUNTBATTEN
PARK AV

BELMONT GDNS
DRYDEN ST

MACKENZIE RD

SHEFFIELD HO
TITTY HO
STREATHER CT
WARWICK
THORPE ST
HOLMES AV
RANDSWAY
NEWTOWN ROAD
SHORTWOODS CL

Raunds

Playing Fields

CLEBURNE WAY
CHERRY WAY
ORCHARD RD
SADDLERS WY
KESTON WY
ANDREWS WAY
MILES CL
HARVEY CL
FRANCIS WAY
CHAMBERLIN WY
McALPINE RD
WELLINGTON ROAD
GROVE ST
CHELVESTON ROAD

FRANCIS TER
STANWICK ROAD
WESTFIELD AV
ANTONA DR
ANTONA GDNS
THE PADDOCK

Darsdale Home

Darsdale Farm

ROAD
B663
CHELVESTON

CHELVESTON
Cemy

INSET 34

NEEDHAM ROAD

DOLBEN AVENUE
MANSFIELD
ALFRED ST
ST LAURENCE ST
RECTORY RD
ADAMS RD
COURTMAN
MANNINGHAM
CLEBURNE RD
POTTER LOVELL
CUMBERLAND AV
CASTLETT
COLLINGS RD
WETENHALL

Club
JOHN EAGLE

RAUNDS ROAD

Primary School

GREEN END
SAMUEL LANE
VILLA LANE
SPENCER PARADE
STREET
HIGH ST
GRANGE ROAD
CHURCH
CHAPEL LA
MANOR GDNS
COURT WOOD

Nursing Home
Hall

Stanwick

The Hall
The Hay Barn
Hall Farm

HILL HOUSE GDNS
ROAD EAST
MARKS CL
NEWBRIDGE
BROOKSIDE
THE

Orch Far

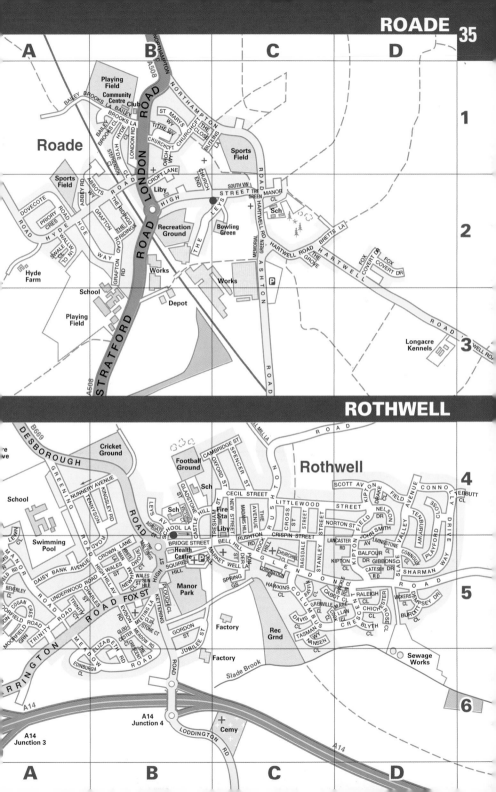

A B C D

Ladywell
Spinney

1

Playing
Field

WHITMORE
CT

KINGSLEY RD

Dove
Farm

CHURCH

LONDON ROAD

TOWCEST

A43

THE
WILLOWS

PUDDLEDOCK

HILLSIDE AVENUE

TOWCESTER

KINGSLEY
RD

KINGSLEY

ROAD

WHITTLEBURY

END

STREET

STOCKS LITTLE HILL

WHITTLEBURY RD

ROAD

WHITTLEBURY ROAD

Silverstone

WEST

Sch

HIGH STREET

FROG
HALL

THE SLADE

2

MONKS-
WOOD

Hazelwood

END

GREEN LANE

HOME CL

WALNUT CL

CHAPEL

ACORN
WY

OLD OAK DR CL

OLD OAK DR

BAINS

Sch

HILL

MURSWELL

ROAD

JUSTINS

ROAD

GRAHAM

STEWART

BRAGHAM

MURSWELL CL

LANE MURSWELL LA

TOWCESTER

3

THE
WOODLANDS

CATTLE

Cattle
End

SAYERS CL

Silverstone
Manor

END

ROAD

THE HAWTHORNS

BRACKLEY

ROAD

DADFORD

Fox
Co

Hick
Cop

4

BRACKLEY ROAD

A43

Bleak Hall
Farmhouse

ROAD

Wild
Wood

P

P

P

Terraces

Copse
Corner

Rally
School

P

Litchlake
Farm

Trade Mall

SILVERSTONE
TECHNOLOGY PARK

Woodcote
Corner

Media
Centre

Bars, Restaurants,
Information & Toilets

5

The
Straights

Brooklands

Luffield

Medical
Centre

Terraces

Luffield

Priory

SILVERSTONE
MOTOR RACING CIRCUIT

Maggotts
Curve

Henhood
Farm

Luffield
Grandstand

Karting
Hall

Bridge
Corner

Luffield Abbey
Farm

B
Gra

6

Terraces

Farm
Straight

Abbey
Curve

Becketts
Corner

Chapel
Curve

Airstrip

Farthing Wood

ROAD

A B C D

TOWCESTER
LACTODORVM

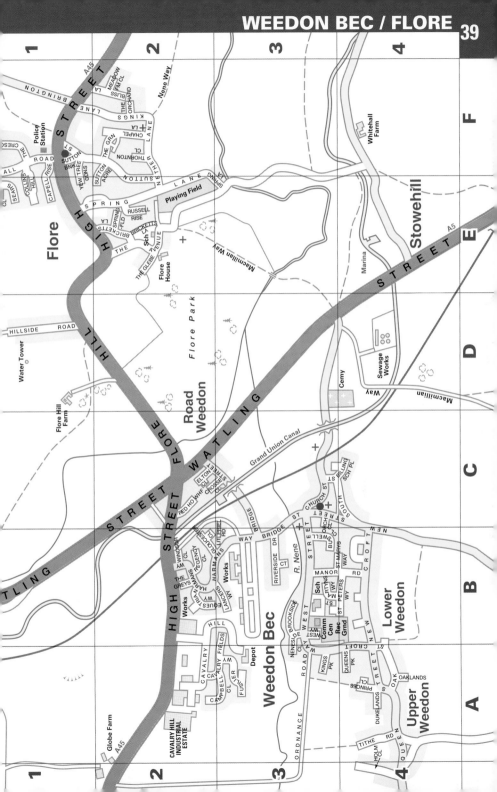

1   **2**   **3**   **4**

F

Flore

E

Stowehill

D

Road Weedon

C

B

Weedon Bec

Lower Weedon

A

Upper Weedon

1   **2**   **3**   **4**

Police Station

Water Tower

Flore Hill Farm

Globe Farm

CAVALRY HILL INDUSTRIAL ESTATE

Whitehall Farm

Marina

Sewage Works

Cemy

Flore Park

Grand Union Canal

R. Nene

Playing Field

Flore House

Comm Cen

Rec Grnd

HILL STREET

HIGH STREET

WATLING STREET

FLORE STREET

STOWEHILL STREET

HILLSIDE ROAD

Macmillan Way

Nene Way

SUTTON ST

A45

A5

The Index includes some names for which there is insufficient space on the maps. These names are indicated by an * and are followed by the nearest adjoining thoroughfare.

Abbey Ct NN29 16 B4
Abbey Rd, Northampton NN7 35 A2
Abbey Rd, Wellingborough NN8 41 E5
Abbey Rise NN29 16 B4
Abbey St, Daventry NN11 19 D5
Abbey St, Northampton NN5 28 A4
Abbey Ter NN5 28 A4
Abbey Way NN10 33 D8
Abbot Cl NN11 19 E7
Abbots Way, Northampton NN7 35 A2
Abbots Way, Wellingborough NN8 40 D4
Abbotts Way, Northampton NN5 28 A3
Abbotts Way, Rushden NN10 33 B7
Aberdare Rd NN5 28 A2
Abington Av NN1 29 F2
Abington Cotts NN1 29 G1
Abington Gro NN1 29 F1
Abington Park Cres NN3 29 H3
Abington Sq NN1 29 E3
Abington St NN1 28 D4
Ablett Cl NN14 37 D6
Ace La NN7 30 E4
Acorn Cl NN14 37 A6
Acorn Way NN12 36 B2
Acre St NN16 25 F5
Adams Av NN1 29 F2
Adams Cl, Stanwick NN9 34 D5
Adams Cl, Wellingborough NN8 41 F2
Adams Dr NN14 35 A5
Addington Rd NN9 22 B4
Addison Rd NN14 17 B3
Adelaide St NN2 28 D2
Adit Vw NN9 22 A6
Admirals Way NN11 19 E6
Adnitt Rd, Northampton NN1 29 F2
Adnitt Rd, Rushden NN10 33 C6
Afan Cl NN16 24 C2
Affleck Bri NN9 16 B2
Aggate Way NN6 20 A5
Agnes Rd NN2 28 D1
Aintree Dr NN10 33 F8
Alastor NN8 40 A3
Albany Rd NN1 29 H2
Albert Pl NN1 29 E4
Albert Rd, Finedon NN9 16 B2
Albert Rd, Rushden NN10 33 D6
Albert Rd, Wellingborough NN8 41 F2
Albert St NN16 25 E5
Albion Ct NN1 29 E4
Albion Pl, Northampton NN1 29 E4
Albion Pl, Rushden NN10 33 E7
Albion Rd NN16 24 D4
Alcombe Rd NN1 29 E3
Alder Cl NN14 17 F3
Alexander Ct NN29 23 C2
Alexander Pl NN9 22 C2
Alexander Rd NN9 22 C1
Alexandra Rd, Corby NN17 14 C2
Alexandra Rd, Kettering NN14 17 B2
Alexandra Rd, Northampton NN1 29 E4
Alexandra Rd, Wellingborough NN8 41 F2
Alexandra St, Burton Latimer NN15 13 D3
Alexandra St, Kettering NN16 25 E5
Alfoxden NN8 40 A5
Alfred St, Irchester NN29 23 B2
Alfred St, Kettering NN16 25 E5
Alfred St, Northampton NN1 29 F4
Alfred St, Rushden NN10 33 D6
Alfred St, Stanwick NN9 34 C6
Alibone Cl NN3 27 B5
Alice Dr NN15 13 D4
Alington Cl NN9 16 C1
Allebone Rd NN6 20 B4
Allen Rd, Finedon NN9 16 C2
Allen Rd, Northampton NN1 29 G2
Allen Rd, Rushden NN10 33 E5
Allen Rd, Wellingborough NN9 22 A5
Allens Gate NN13 12 A4
Alliance Ct NN8 41 E3
Alliance Ter NN8 41 E3
Alliston Gdns NN2 28 D2
Alma St, Northampton NN5 28 A4
Alma St, Wellingborough NN8 41 E3
Almond Cl NN7 30 F3
Almond Rd NN16 24 F4
Alpine Rd NN10 33 B6
Altendiez Way NN15 13 C1
Althorp Rd NN5 28 B4
Alvis Way NN11 18 A4
Ambleside Cl NN8 40 B2
Ambush St NN5 28 B4
Amundsen Cl NN11 18 C2
Anderson Grn NN8 40 A4
Andrew Cl NN10 32 E1
Andrews Way NN9 34 A4
Angel La NN8 41 E3
Angel St NN1 28 D4
Anglian Rd NN11 19 B5
Annandale Rd NN17 14 B1
Anne Cl NN10 32 E1
Anne Rd NN8 40 C6
Anne St NN17 14 C3
Anson Cl NN11 19 E6
Antona Cl NN9 34 A5
Antona Dr NN9 34 A4
Antona Gdns NN9 34 A5
Apollo Cl NN11 18 B3
Appletree Ct NN9 16 B2
Archery Rd OX17 27 C2
Archfield NN8 40 D4
Archfield Ter NN9 22 B3
Arden Cl NN11 18 C3
Ardington Rd NN1 29 G2
Argyle St NN5 28 A3
Argyll St, Corby NN17 14 C2
Argyll St, Kettering NN15 25 D7
Arkwright Rd NN29 23 C2
Armley Cl NN6 23 C4
Arnills Way CV23 26 B3
Arnold Rd NN2 28 D1
Arnsby Cres NN3 27 A5
Arnull Cres NN11 18 C3
Arrow Cl OX17 27 C2
Arrow Head Rd NN4 28 A6
Arthingworth Rd NN14 17 A2
Arthur St, Northampton NN2 28 D1
Arthur St, Wellingborough NN8 40 D4
Arthur Ter*, Arthur St NN2 28 D1
Arthurs Walk*, Alexandra St NN16 25 E5
Artizan Rd NN1 29 F2
Arundel Cl, Banbury OX17 26 B5
Arundel Cl, Kettering NN14 37 E6
Arundel Ct NN10 33 C8
Arundel St NN1 28 C3
Ascot Rd NN10 33 F8
Ash Cl, Daventry NN11 18 D2
Ash Cl, Wellingborough NN29 23 C3
Ash Ct NN14 37 D8
Ash Dr NN13 12 C2
Ash Gro, Bugbrooke NN7 30 E4
Ash Gro, Kettering NN14 17 A2
Ash Rd NN15 25 F6
Ash St NN1 28 D3
Ash Tree Ct OX17 27 D2
Ashbourne Dr NN14 17 A2
Ashbrow Rd NN4 28 A6
Ashburnham Rd NN1 29 G1
Ashby Ct, Kislingbury NN7 21 C5
Ashby Ct, Northampton NN3 27 B6
Ashby Dr, Northampton NN6 15 C3
Ashby Dr, Rushden NN10 33 C8
Ashby Gdns NN3 27 B6
Ashby Pk NN11 18 C3
Ashby Rd, Daventry NN11 18 C2
Ashby Rd, Daventry NN11 18 C1
Ashby Rd, Rugby CV23 26 B2
Ashdown Pl NN17 14 C1
Ashdown Rd NN11 18 D3
Ashfield Av NN9 34 B3
Ashfield Rd NN8 40 C4
Ashfield Rs NN9 34 B3
Ashford Lea NN14 17 A2
Ashgate Ct NN14 35 B4
Ashlade OX17 27 D3
Ashley Ct NN16 24 C4
Ashley La NN3 27 C5
Ashridge Cl NN10 33 C8
Ashton Cl NN11 18 B3
Ashton Rd, Northampton NN7 35 C2
Ashton Rd, Peterborough PE8 31 C4
Ashwell Rd NN10 33 F6
Ashwin Cl NN13 12 B2
Ashworth Cl NN6 15 C2
Ashworth St NN11 19 D6
Askham Av NN8 40 C6
Aspen Cl NN10 33 D5
Astbury Cl NN11 19 D7
Aster Rd NN16 24 F3
Astrop Gdns OX17 26 C5
Astrop Grange OX17 26 C5
Astrop Rd, King's Sutton OX17 26 B6
Astrop Rd, Middleton Cheney OX17 27 C3
Athelstan Rd NN16 25 F5
Attley Ct NN8 40 B3
Attley Way NN9 22 C3
Auctioneers Ct NN1 28 D5
Auctioneers Way NN1 28 D5
Austin Cl NN29 23 D2
Austin Ho*, High St NN14 35 B5
Austin St NN1 29 E2
Austin Way NN11 18 A3
Austins Pl NN12 36 B2
Austins Yd NN6 20 B3
Avalon Ct*, Cross St NN14 35 C4
Avenue Bernard NN13 12 B3
Avenue Cl NN9 16 A2
Avenue Rd, Finedon NN9 16 A2
Avenue Rd, Wellingborough NN8 41 E2
Avon Cl, Daventry NN11 19 A6
Avon Cl, Kettering NN16 24 C3
Avon Cl, Wellingborough NN8 40 B1
Avonbury Ct NN13 12 D6
Avondale Rd NN16 24 E4
Axe Head Rd NN4 28 A6
Aynsley Cl NN14 17 B3

Backley Cl NN15 25 A7
Backway NN29 16 C5
Badby Pk NN11 18 B2
Badby Rd NN11 19 C6
Badby Rd West NN11 19 B7
Baden Powell Cres NN12 38 B5
Badgers Cl NN7 30 E3
Baffin Cl NN14 35 C5
Bailey Brooks Cl NN7 35 B1
Bailey Brooks La NN7 35 A1
Bailey Ct NN10 32 D3
Bailiff St NN1 28 D3
Bains Cl NN12 36 B2
Baird Cl NN11 18 C2
Baird Ct NN8 40 A2
Bairstow Rd NN12 38 C5
Bakehouse La*, Kettering Rd NN15 13 E2
Baker Cres NN29 23 B2
Baker Ct NN14 37 D7
Baker St, Irthlingborough NN9 22 A5
Baker St, Northampton NN2 28 C2
Baker St, Wellingborough NN8 41 E2
Bakers Ct NN14 37 A6
Baler Cl NN11 18 D1
Balfour Dr NN14 35 D5
Balfour Rd NN2 28 D1
Balfour St NN16 24 E3
Balham Cl NN10 33 B8
Ballantyne Rd NN10 33 C7
Balliol Rd, Brackley NN13 12 A3
Balliol Rd, Daventry NN11 19 C7
Balmoral Av NN10 33 E5
Balmoral Cl, Northampton NN6 20 C4
Balmoral Cl, Towcester NN12 38 B5
Balmoral Cl, Wellingborough NN8 40 C6
Balmoral Dr NN13 12 B3
Balmoral Way OX17 26 B5
Bampton Ct NN18 14 D4
Banbury La, King's Sutton OX17 26 A4
Banbury La, Middleton Cheney OX17 27 A2
Banbury Rd NN13 12 A4
Banner Cl NN10 33 C7
Bannerman Dr NN13 12 A4
Barby Rd CV23 26 A2
Baring Rd NN5 28 B3
Barker Cl NN10 33 E6
Barker Rd NN6 20 B4
Barley Cft NN6 15 C1
Barley Cl NN11 18 D1
Barley Ct NN10 33 E7
Barlow Cl NN14 35 A4
Barlow La NN3 27 B5
Barnes Cl, Daventry NN11 18 C4
Barnes Cl, Kettering NN15 25 E8
Barnett Rd OX17 27 B3
Barnwell Cl NN14 37 E6
Barnwell Dr NN10 33 C8
Barnwell Rd, Peterborough PE8 31 B4
Barnwell Rd, Wellingborough NN8 40 B1
Barnwell St NN16 25 F5
Baron Av, Kettering NN16 24 A4
Baron Av, Northampton NN6 20 B2
Baronson Gdns NN1 29 G2
Barrack Rd NN2 28 D2
Barret Cl NN8 40 A3
Barrett Cl NN10 32 E3
Barringers Gdns NN29 23 C1
Barrington Ct NN13 12 C6
Barrington Rd NN10 33 E8
Barry Rd NN1 29 G3
Bartlett Ct NN13 12 A4
Bartley Dr NN16 24 B4
Barton Cl OX17 26 B5
Barton Rd NN15 25 F8
Barwick Ho NN10 33 D6
Bassett Ford Rd PE8 31 C5
Bassett Pl PE8 31 C4
Bassett's Cl NN8 40 D3
Bassett's Ct NN8 40 D3
Bates Cl NN10 32 D3
Bath La NN16 24 E4
Bath Rd NN16 24 E2
Baulmsholme Cl NN4 28 D6
Bayard Brow NN13 12 B3
Bayes St NN16 24 C4
Baysdale Av NN17 14 C2
Beaconsfield Pl NN10 33 D5
Beaconsfield Ter NN1 29 E2
Beaconsfield Ter*, Rectory Rd NN10 33 D5
Beanfield Av NN18 14 A3
Beardsley Ct NN18 14 B4
Beatrice Rd NN16 24 D3
Beatty Cl NN11 19 F6
Beaumaris Cl NN10 33 F7
Beaumont Cl NN16 24 D1
Beaumont Cres NN13 12 B4
Beck Ct NN8 40 B2
Beckets Vw NN1 29 E5
Bedale Rd NN8 41 E2
Bede Cl NN10 32 E3
Bedford Pl NN1 29 E4
Bedford Rd, Northampton NN1 29 E5
Bedford Rd, Rushden NN10 33 E7
Beech Av NN3 29 H1
Beech Cl, Kettering NN14 17 C3
Beech Cl, Northampton NN7 30 E3
Beech Cl, Towcester NN12 38 B6
Beech Cres, Kettering NN15 25 F6
Beech Cres, Wellingborough NN29 23 C3
Beech Ct NN14 37 D7
Beech Dr, Brackley NN13 12 B1
Beech Dr, Wellingborough NN8 40 C3
Beech Gro NN10 33 B5
Beech La NN7 21 D4
Beech Rd NN10 32 D4
Beechwood Suite NN8 41 G4
Beeston Pl NN18 14 A3
Bell Ct, Corby NN18 1
Bell Ct, Wellingborough NN8 4
Bell End NN29 1
Bell Hill, Kettering NN14 3
Bell Hill, Wellingborough NN9
Bell St NN8 4
Bellamy Rd PE8 3
Belle Baulk NN12 3
Belmont Gdns NN9 3
Belvedere Cl NN5 2
Belvedere Rd NN15 2
Belvoir Cl NN10 3
Benbow Cl NN11
Benedict Cl NN10 3
Benefield Rd PE8 3
Bengeworth Ct NN8 4
Bennett Cl NN11 1
Bentley Walk NN18 1
Bentley Way NN11 1
Berkeley Cl NN1 2
Bern Links NN4 2
Bernside NN4 2
Berrill St NN29 2
Berrister Pl NN9 3
Berry Cl NN6 2
Berry Green Ct NN9 1
Berry Green Rd NN9 1
Berry Green Ter*, Berry Green La NN9 1
Berryfield NN6 2
Berrymoor Ct NN8 4
Berrymoor Rd NN8 4
Bessemer Gro NN17
Bestwood Grn NN18 1
Betjeman Cl, Daventry NN11 1
Betjeman Cl, Rushden NN10 3
Betony Walk NN10 3
Beverley Cl NN14 3
Beverley Rd NN15 2
Beverley Walk*, Thirsk Rd NN18 1
Bewick Ct NN18 1
Bibury Cl NN8 4
Bickerstaffes Rd NN12 3
Bidders Cl NN1 2
Bideford Sq NN18 1
Bignal Cl NN15 2
Billing La NN6 2
Billing Rd NN1 2
Billing School Pl NN7 3
Billington St NN1 2
Bilsdon Cl NN10 3
Bilton Ct NN8 4
Bingham Walk NN18 1
Birch Av NN18 1
Birch Rd, Kettering NN16 2
Birch Rd, Rushden NN10 3
Birchall Rd NN10 3
Birchfield Rd, Northampton NN1 2
Birchfield Rd, Wellingborough NN8 4
Birchfield Rd East NN3 2
Birchvale Ct NN14 1
Bird St NN15 1
Birkdale Cl NN11 1
Birkdale Dr NN10 3
Bishops Cl NN13 1
Bishops Ct, Daventry NN11 1
Bishops Ct, Rushden NN10 3
Bishops Dr NN15 2
Black Lion Hill NN1 2
Black Pot La PE8 3
Blackberry Cl NN16 2
Blackberry La NN4 2
Blackbird Cl NN13 1
Blackfriars NN10 3
Blackmoor Av NN18 1
Blackthorn Cl NN16 2
Blackwell Cl NN12 3
Blake Cl NN11 1
Blake Rd NN18 1
Blake Walk NN10 3
Blanford Av NN16 2
Blaydon Walk NN8 4
Bleaklow Cl NN14 1
Blencowe Dr NN13 1
Blenheim Cft NN13 1
Blenheim Cl NN10 3
Blenheim Rd NN8 4
Blenheim Rise OX17 2
Blinco Rd NN10 3
Bliss La NN7 3
Blisworth Rd NN7 3
Bloomfield Cl NN10 3
Bluebell Rise NN10 3
Blyth Cl NN14 3

ton Ct NN18 14 A4
ard St NN9 22 B4
ardman Rd NN15 25 B7
at Horse La NN6 15 C3
ddington Rd NN15 25 E7
ddington Way NN13 12 A3
diam Cl NN14 37 E6
dleian Cl NN11 13 D7
tons Cl NN13 12 B2
nham Ct NN16 24 E4
nnington Walk NN18 14 B4
rough Ct*,
Westfields Av NN10 32 D3
rough Rd NN13 12 C6
rookdale Rd NN17 14 B1
stock Av NN1 29 F2
ston Cl NN18 14 A4
swell La MK19 15 A5
ughton Dr NN10 33 C7
ughton Rd NN3 27 A5
undary Av NN10 33 A6
undary Rd NN13 12 C6
urne Cl NN8 40 A2
averie Walk NN1 29 F3
wden Rd NN5 28 B4
wen Sq NN15 19 D5
whill NN16 25 B6
wlers Yd NN6 20 B3
wling Green Av NN15 25 D6
wling Green Rd NN15 25 D6
wman Cl OX17 27 C2
wness NN8 40 B3
k Gdns NN8 41 E2
xwood Dr CV23 26 B2
abham Cl NN12 36 B2
acken Cl NN16 24 D2
ackley Fields Cotts N13 12 B1
ackley Grange Cotts N13 12 A1
ackley Lodge Mews N13 12 B4
ackley Rd, Ilverstone NN12 36 A4
ackley Rd, owcester NN12 38 A4
acknell NN8 40 A3
dfield Cl NN10 33 F5
dmore Gdns NN18 14 A3
adshaw St NN1 28 D4
adshaw Way NN3 23 B2
aggintons La OX17 27 D3
aid Ct NN8 40 B1
aithwaite Cl NN15 25 B7
amble Cl NN16 24 D1
amble Rd NN12 38 A5
ambleside, ettering NN16 24 D2
ambleside, rapston NN14 37 D7
ambleside Ct NN16 24 D2
amley Cl NN10 33 B5
amley Ct NN29 16 B4
amshill Av NN16 24 C2
amston Cl PE8 31 C4
ngWayn Walk NN18 14 B4
ansons La NN12 38 C4
asenose Dr NN13 12 A3
aunston Rd NN11 18 A3
aunton Pl NN18 14 D4
wn Cl NN9
ybrooke Rd NN14 17 A2
ayford Av NN18 14 D4
eakleys Rd NN14 17 D3
econ Cl NN16 24 D1
econ St NN5 28 B2
eezehill Way NN8 41 E1
ent Cl NN16 13 C3
entford NN8 40 A3
etts La NN7 35 C2
win Cl NN13 12 A2
ar Cl NN11 12 C2
ar Ct NN9 22 B5
ar Wood Way NN29 16 B6
ary Cl NN12 38 B6
k Kiln Cl NN12 38 C5
k Kiln La NN2 28 D1
k Kiln Rd NN9 34 B1
cketts La NN7 39 E2
ckhill Mews NN8 40 D3
ckhill Rd NN8 40 B4
dewell La*, orse Mkt NN16 25 D5
dge Ct, Corby NN17 14 E1
dge Ct, ettering NN14 37 C7
dge Rd NN14 17 B2
dge St, Brackley NN13 12 B5
dge St, orthampton NN1 28 D4
dge St, othwell NN14 35 B5
dge St, rapston NN14 37 B7
dge St, Weedon NN7 39 B3
dge Ct, ellingborough NN9 34 C2
dgewater Cl NN13 12 C3
dgewater Cres NN13 12 C3
dgewater NN13 12 C2

Bridgewater Mews NN13 12 C3
Bridgewater Rd NN13 12 B2
Bridgewater Rise NN13 12 C3
Bridgford Pl NN18 14 A3
Bridle Rd NN15 13 C2
Brigg Ct NN18 14 A4
Brighouse Cl NN18 14 A4
Brindley Cl, Daventry NN11 18 A2
Brindley Ct, Rushden NN10 32 B4
Brington Rd, Flore NN7 39 F1
Brington Rd, Long Buckby NN6 23 B5
Brinsley Grn NN18 14 A2
Britannia Gdns NN8 41 G4
Britannia Rd NN16 24 D3
British La*, School La NN16 25 D5
Briton Gdns NN3 29 H1
Briton Rd NN3 29 H1
Briton Ter NN3, 29 H1
Brixham Walk*, Burghley Dr NN18 14 D4
Broad March Rd NN11 19 E6
Broad St, Earls Barton NN8 20 B3
Broad St, Northampton NN1 28 D3
Broadlands, Kettering NN14 17 D4
Broadlands, Rushden NN10 33 E5
Broadlands, Wellingborough NN9 34 C3
Broadwater La NN12 38 A4
Broadway, Kettering NN15 25 D7
Broadway, Northampton NN1 29 G1
Broadway, Wellingborough NN8 41 E5
Brockhall Rd NN7 39 E1
Bronte Cl NN16 24 E1
Brook La, Northampton NN5 29 G1
Brook La, Towcester NN12 38 A4
Brook St, Daventry NN11 19 C5
Brook St, Daventry NN11 19 D5
Brook St, Northampton NN1 28 C3
Brook St, Wellingborough NN9 34 C3
Brook St East NN8 41 F3
Brook St West NN8 40 D4
Brook Ter NN9 22 B3
Brook Vale NN8 40 B6
Brook Way MK19 15 A6
Brooke Cl, Rushden NN10 33 D7
Brooke Cl, Wellingborough NN8 40 A3
Brooke Grn NN8 40 A2
Brooke Mews NN8 40 A2
Brookfield Rd NN10 33 C6
Brookland Cres NN1 29 G1
Brooklands Cl NN11 19 D6
Brooks Cl NN16 13 E4
Brooks Rd NN9 34 D2
Brooksdale Cl NN16 24 D1
Brookside, Kettering NN14 17 D4
Brookside, Northampton NN7 39 B3
Brookside, Wellingborough NN8 34 D6
Brookside Pl NN7 30 B1
Broom Way NN15 25 B7
Browning Av NN16 24 E2
Browning Cl NN11 18 C3
Browning Rd NN8 40 A3
Browns Cl NN3 27 B4
Browns Way NN1 29 F5
Browns Yd, Northampton NN7 30 E4
Browns Yd, Towcester NN12 38 B3
Bruce St NN5 18 A3
Brunel Cl, Daventry NN11 18 A3
Brunel Cl, Kettering NN16 24 C4
Brunel Cl, Wellingborough NN8 40 A1
Brunswick Pl NN11 29 F3
Brunting Rd NN3 27 A6
Bryant Rd NN15 25 E8
Bryant Way NN10 32 D2
Buccleuch St NN16 24 C4
Buckfast Sq NN18 14 D4
Buckingham Cl NN8 40 D6
Buckingham Ct NN13 12 C5
Buckingham Rd, Brackley NN13 12 C4
Buckingham Rd, Milton Keynes MK19 15 B6
Buckingham Rd Ind Est NN13 12 C5

Buckingham Way NN12 38 A5
Bucknills La NN6 15 B2
Buckwell Cl, Kettering NN16 17 C3
Buckwell Cl, Wellingborough NN8 40 D3
Buckwell End NN8 40 D3
Buckwell Pl NN8 40 D3
Bugbrooke Rd, Kislingbury NN7 21 B6
Bugbrooke Rd, Nether Heyford NN7 30 A1
Bugby Dr NN9 22 D1
Bugby Way NN9 34 C2
Bull Baulk OX17 27 C2
Bulls Cl NN15 26 B5
Bunting Cl NN15 13 C3
Bunting Rd NN2 28 D1
Burcote Flds NN12 38 C5
Burcote Rd NN12 38 C5
Burditt Cl NN14 35 D5
Burford Way NN8 40 B6
Burghley Cl, Corby NN18 14 D4
Burghley Cl, Kettering NN14 17 C2
Burghley Dr NN18 14 D3
Burghley St NN16 24 E3
Burleigh Ho*, Rectory Ct NN10 33 D6
Burns Cl NN6 20 C4
Burns Rd, Daventry NN11 18 C3
Burns Rd, Kettering NN16 24 E2
Burns Rd, Wellingborough NN8 40 A4
Burns St NN1 29 E2
Burton Cl NN11 18 C2
Burton Latimer By-Pass NN15 13 F1
Burton Rd NN9 16 B1
Burwell Hill NN13 12 C3
Burwell Hill Cl NN13 12 C3
Bury Cl NN10 32 E2
Bury Dyke NN6 15 C2
Burystead Pl NN8 41 E4
Burystead Rise NN9 34 C2
Bush Acre Ct NN16 24 B4
Bush Cl NN8 40 D3
Buswell Cl NN7 39 B3
Butlin Cl, Daventry NN11 14 C2
Butlin Cl, Kettering NN14 35 A5
Butlin Ct NN8 41 G6
Butlins La NN7 35 B1
Butterfields NN8 41 E6
Buttermere NN8 40 A3
Buttermere Cl NN16 25 A5
Butts Hill Cres NN7 30 F3
Butts Rd, Raunds NN9 34 C2
Butts Rd, Wellingborough NN8 40 D6
Buxton Dr NN14 17 A2
Byfield Rd NN5 28 B4
Byron Cl NN12 38 A5
Byron Cres, Knuston NN10 33 A5
Byron Cres, Warmonds Hill NN10 32 D3
Byron Rd, Kettering NN16 24 E3
Byron Rd, Wellingborough NN8 40 B4
Byron St NN2 29 F1
Byron Walk NN11 18 C3

Cabot Cl, Daventry NN11 18 D2
Cabot Cl, Kettering NN14 35 C5
Caernarvon Cl NN14 38 B5
Caesars Gate NN13 12 D5
Cambium Cl NN11 24 E1
Cambridge St, Kettering NN14 35 B4
Cambridge St, Northampton NN2 28 C2
Cambridge St, Rothwell NN14 24 E4
Cambridge St, Wellingborough NN8 41 E3
Cameron Cl NN11 19 C6
Cameron Ct NN17 14 D3
Camp Hill NN7 30 E4
Camp La NN7 21 D5
Campbell Cl, Northampton NN7 39 A2
Campbell Cl, Towcester NN12 38 C2
Campbell Rd, Corby NN17 14 D3
Campbell Rd, Wellingborough NN8 41 E6
Campbell Sq NN6 20 A3
Campbell Sq*, Church La NN1 28 D3
Campbell St NN1 28 D3
Camrose Rd NN5 28 B2
Cannon St NN8 41 F3
Canon St NN16 25 E5

Canonbury NN8 40 A4
Capell Gdns NN18 14 C4
Capell Rise NN7 39 E1
Cappenham Cl NN12 38 B3
Cardigan Cl NN5 28 A2
Cardigan Pl NN16 25 F5
Carey Cl NN3 27 A5
Carey Ct NN3 27 A6
Carey Dr NN17 14 A1
Carey Rd NN12 38 B6
Carey St, Kettering NN16 25 E5
Carey St, Northampton NN1 29 E2
Carey Way NN10 33 F5
Carlton Cl NN10 33 C8
Carlton Mews NN10 33 E3
Carlton St NN16 25 C5
Carmarthen Way NN10 33 F8
Carnegie St NN10 33 C6
Carradale Cl NN16 24 C2
Carriage Dr NN16 24 D1
Carrington St NN16 25 D5
Carrs Way NN7 21 C2
Carsington Cl NN16 24 A4
Carter Cl NN8 41 F3
Cartmel Way NN10 33 F5
Cartrill St NN9 34 B3
Cartwright Cres NN13 12 A4
Cartwright Rd NN12 38 C4
Casterton Cl NN9 34 D5
Castilian St NN1 29 E4
Castilian Ter NN1 29 E4
Castle Ct, Daventry NN11 19 C6
Castle Cl, Rushden NN10 33 D8
Castle Ct, Wellingborough NN8 41 F4
Castle Hill, Daventry NN11 19 C6
Castle Hill, Kettering NN14 35 B5
Castle La NN8 41 F4
Castle Mews NN8 41 F4
Castle Mnt NN13 12 B6
Castle Rd NN14 17 A2
Castle St, Northampton NN1 28 C4
Castle St, Wellingborough NN8 41 F4
Castle Way NN8 41 F4
Catesby Rd NN14 35 D5
Catesby St NN16 24 E4
Catlow Cl NN9 34 B1
Cattle Market Rd NN1 28 D5
Cavalry Dr NN11 19 B5
Cavalry Flds NN7 39 A2
Cavalry Hill NN7 39 A2
Cavalry Hill Ind Est NN7 39 A2
Caxton Cl NN11 18 A3
Cecil Cl NN18 14 C4
Cecil St NN18 14 C4
Cecil St, Kettering NN16 24 E3
Cecil St, Rothwell NN14 35 C4
Cedar Cl, Brackley NN13 12 C1
Cedar Cl, Daventry NN11 18 D2
Cedar Cl, Kettering NN14 17 C3
Cedar Cl, Rushden NN10 33 D8
Cedar Cl, Towcester NN12 38 B6
Cedar Cl, Wellingborough NN8 23 B3
Cedar Dr NN14 37 C7
Cedar Rd, Kettering NN16 24 E3
Cedar Rd, Northampton NN1 29 G1
Cedar Rd East NN3 29 H1
Cedar Way, Rushden NN10 32 D2
Cedar Way, Wellingborough NN8 41 E1
Cemetery La NN10 32 E2
Centaine Rd NN10 33 C7
Central Av, Kettering NN16 24 F4
Central Av, Wellingborough NN8 40 C6
Centre Par NN6 15 C2
Chace Rd NN8 41 G4
Chacombe Rd OX17 27 C1
Chaffinch Way NN13 12 B2
Chalk La NN1 28 C4
Chamberlain Av, Rushden NN10 40 D6
Chamberlain Way, Rushden NN10 32 E3
Chamberlain Way, Wellingborough NN8 34 B4
Champion Ct NN13 12 B3
Chancery La NN14 37 C6
Chandler Gdns NN14 37 D7
Channing St NN16 25 E5
Chantelle Ct NN11 18 C3
Chantry La NN11 18 C3
Chapel Cl NN12 36 B2
Chapel Hill, Kettering NN14 37 B6
Chapel Hill, Rushden NN10 32 D1

Chapel Hill, Wellingborough NN29 23 C2
Chapel La, Corby NN17 14 F2
Chapel La, Daventry NN11 19 D5
Chapel La, Flore NN7 39 F2
Chapel La, Northampton NN6 15 C2
Chapel La, Wellingborough NN9 34 D6
Chapel Pl NN1 29 E3
Chapel St CV23 26 B2
Chaplins La NN14 17 D3
Chapman Cl NN12 38 B2
Chapman Gro NN17 14 C1
Chapmans Cl NN29 23 C3
Charles Cl, Northampton NN6 23 B5
Charles Cl, Rushden NN10 32 E1
Charles Partridge Ct NN8 40 A6
Charles Robinson Ct NN8 40 C4
Charles St, Kettering NN16 24 D3
Charles St, Northampton NN1 28 D3
Charles St, Rothwell NN8 35 A5
Charles St, Thrapston NN14 37 D6
Charles St, Wellingborough NN8 40 C6
Charles St*, Elizabeth St NN17 14 C3
Charles Ter NN11 19 D6
Charnwood Cl NN11 18 C3
Charnwood Rd NN17 14 C2
Charterhouse Cl NN13 12 B4
Chatellebault Ct NN17 14 B1
Chater St NN3 27 B5
Chaucer Rd NN8 40 B4
Chaucer Way NN11 19 C5
Chelmorton Vale NN14 17 A2
Cheltenham Cl NN10 33 F7
Chelveston Rd, Raunds NN9 34 B4
Chelveston Rd, Rushden NN10 32 F2
Chelveston Rd, Stanwick NN9 34 D6
Cheney Ct OX17 27 C2
Cheney Gdns OX17 27 B1
Chepstow Cl NN8 28 B2
Chequers La NN8 41 E3
Cheriton Cl NN11 18 D1
Cheriton Rd NN14 14 D4
Cherradene Ct NN9 34 C3
Cherry Av NN8 41 E1
Cherry Cl NN9 22 A5
Cherry Orch NN10 33 E7
Cherry Rd NN16 24 F3
Cherry St NN9 22 A5
Cherry Tree Cl NN14 17 D3
Cherry Way NN9 34 A4
Cherwell Banks OX17 26 B4
Chester Av NN7 21 A2
Chester Rd, Irchester NN29 23 C1
Chester Rd, Rushden NN10 33 B6
Chester Rd, Wellingborough NN8 41 G3
Chestnut Av NN15 25 E6
Chestnut Cl NN10 33 B5
Chestnut Dr, Brackley NN13 12 B1
Chestnut Dr, Desborough NN14 17 E3
Chestnut Dr, Thrapston NN14 37 C7
Chestnut Gro NN15 25 E7
Cheviot Cl NN16 24 D1
Cheyne Walk NN1 29 E4
Chichele Cl NN10 32 E3
Chichele St NN10 33 D5
Chichele St NN10 32 E2
Chicheley Cotts NN14 37 C7
Chichester Cl, Daventry NN11 19 E5
Chichester Cl, Kettering NN16 35 D5
Chiltern Rd, Daventry NN11 18 C2
Chiltern Rd, Kettering NN16 24 D2
Chipsey Av, Bugbrooke NN7 30 E3
Chipsey Av, Northampton NN1 29 H4
Chowns Mill Bsns Pk NN9 22 D6
Christchurch Dr NN11 19 C7
Christchurch Rd NN1 29 G3
Christie Way NN15 25 B7
Christine Ct NN9 34 C3
Church Av OX17 26 B6
Church End NN7 35 B1
Church Hall Rd NN10 33 B7

on Dr NN16 24 C3
y Rd NN15 13 D4
ng Ter NN10 13 D5
St NN1 29 E3
Av,
ton Latimer NN15 13 D2
Av, Corby NN17 14 D3
Av, Kettering NN15 25 F5
Cres NN10 33 B6
Gro NN10 33 D5
Langham Rd NN9 34 C2
Rd PE8 31 C3
St, Irchester NN29 23 C2
St,
ng Buckby NN6 23 C4
St,
rthampton NN1 29 G3
St, Stanwick NN9 34 D6
tbrook Hill NN14 17 F3
tern Way NN11 19 D5
field Cres NN9 16 C1
field Rd,
llingborough NN9 22 B4
field Rd,
llingborough NN8 41 G2
field Rd,
allaston NN29 16 B5
hill Cl NN13 12 C4
lands Rd NN6 31 C1
wood Rd PE8 31 C3
Vale Rd NN9 22 A5
n St NN1 29 E4
Grn NN14 17 A2
Cl NN11 19 A5
St NN16 25 D5
r Rd NN16 24 F4
ewood NN13 12 C2
ell St NN16 25 E5
rburgh Cl NN14 33 A6
rburgh Rd,
ttering NN16 24 F4
rburgh Rd,
llingborough NN8 40 C6
rgh Sq NN11 18 C4
n St NN1 29 F3
nonds Cl NN8 41 F6
und St NN16 25 F5
ard Cl,
shden NN10 32 F2
ard Rd,
ettering NN15 25 E8
ard Rd,
llingborough NN29 23 C3
ards Dr NN8 40 C3
ton Cl NN13 12 C4
r Cl, Daventry NN11 18 D3
r Cl, Kettering NN15 13 C3
Ct NN10 33 A5
r Dr NN11 18 D3
n Cl NN6 15 B2
n La NN6 15 A2
n Way NN6 15 A2
St NN5 28 A3
Cl NN16 24 E1
Way NN10 32 C3
abeth Cl,
rthampton NN6 20 B2
beth Cl,
llingborough NN8 40 C6
beth Rd NN10 32 E1
ventry NN11 18 C4
beth Rd,
ttering NN16 24 F4
beth Rd,
hwell NN14 35 B6
St NN17 14 C3
beth Walk NN11 29 F3
beth Way,
rthampton NN6 20 A2
beth Way,
shden NN10 32 E1
beth Way,
llingborough NN9 22 A6
Cl NN6 15 C2
smere Av NN13 12 C2
smere Cl NN13 12 C2
smere Cres NN13 12 C2
smere Ct NN13 12 C2
smere Rd NN13 12 C2
Way NN8 34 B2
Ct NN14 37 D8
Dr, Brackley NN13 12 B2
Dr,
ton Keynes MK19 15 A5
Rd,
ton Latimer NN15 13 E1
Rd, Kettering NN15 25 F6
St,
rthampton NN1 28 D3
St,
llingborough NN8 40 D2
en Rd NN8 41 G3
Cl NN7 39 C2
n Ter NN2 28 D1

Emerald Way NN1 28 C5
Emmanuel Cl,
Daventry NN11 19 C7
Ennerdale Cl,
Daventry NN11 19 B5
Ennerdale Cl,
Kettering NN16 25 C6
Ennerdale Rd NN10 33 F5
Ensleigh Cl NN15 13 E4
Enterprise Cl NN16 24 B3
Enterprise Rd NN9 34 C2
Epping Walk NN11 18 C3
Epsom Cl NN10 33 F7
Equestrian Way NN7 39 B3
Equity Ho NN8 41 G4
Ericsson Cl NN11 18 D2
Eskdaill St NN16 25 D5
Eskdale Av NN17 14 C1
Eskdale Cl NN8 40 B2
Essen La CV23 26 B2
Essex Rd NN10 33 E7
Essex St NN2 28 C1
Ethel St NN1 29 F3
Ettrick Cl NN16 24 C2
Euston Rd NN4 28 C6
Evans Cl NN11 19 E6
Evelyn Way NN29 23 D3
Evensford Walk NN9 22 A6
Everdon Pk NN11 18 B2
Everest La NN17 14 C2
Everitt Cl NN8 41 F5
Evison Rd NN14 35 B5
Ewenfield Rd NN9 16 B3
Excelsior Ct NN9 22 A4
Exeter Cl NN11 19 D7
Exeter Pl NN1 29 F3
Exeter St NN16 24 E3
Exmouth Av NN18 14 D4
Express Cl NN9 22 A6
Eyam Cl NN14 17 A2
Eynard Impasse NN13 12 B2
Eynon Cl NN3 27 A5

Fair La NN14 37 E5
Fairfield Rd NN14 13 A4
Fairhurst Way NN6 20 B3
Fairmead Cres NN10 33 C8
Fairoaks Dr NN9 34 B2
Falcon Way NN13 12 A1
Falconers Cl NN11 18 A3
Fallowfields NN6 15 C2
Faraday Cl NN11 18 B3
Faraday Ct NN14 37 D7
Farm Rd NN14 12 C5
Farmers Dr NN13 12 A3
Farmfield Cl NN15 13 B1
Farnborough Dr NN11 18 B1
Farndale Av NN17 14 B2
Farndish Cl NN10 33 B6
Farndish Rd NN29 23 C2
Farnham Dr NN13 33 B8
Farthinghoe Cl NN13 12 A4
Faugere Cl NN13 12 B3
Feast Field Cl NN9 16 B6
Federation Av NN14 17 B4
Fell Walk NN8 40 B1
Fellows Cl NN29 16 A5
Fenners Cl NN10 33 F6
Fenton Rise NN13 12 A3
Fern Rd NN10 33 C6
Fernie Way NN8 40 C4
Fernmoor Dr NN9 22 B4
Ferrers Cl NN16 32 F1
Ferrestone Rd NN8 41 E2
Fetter St NN1 28 D5
Fettledine Rd NN9 22 D1
Field St NN16 24 D4
Field Street Av NN16 24 D4
Field Vw NN13 12 A4
Fields Vw NN8 41 F4
Fife St NN5 28 A3
Finedon Rd,
Irthlingborough NN9 22 A3
Finedon Rd,
Kettering NN15 13 D4
Finedon Rd,
Wellingborough NN8 41 F2
Finedon St NN15 13 D3
Fineshade Gro NN17 14 C1
Fir Rd NN16 25 F5
First Av NN8 32 D4
First La NN5 28 A4
Fish St NN1 28 D4
Fisher Cl,
Kettering NN16 37 D7
Fisher Cl, Rugby CV23 26 B3
Fishton Cl NN15 25 E8
Fitzroy Pl NN1 28 C4
Fitzwilliam Leys NN15 32 D1
Fitzwilliam Rd NN9 22 B3
Fitzwilliam St NN10 33 D6
Flavius Gate NN13 12 D4
Fleet St NN16 25 C5
Fletcher Gdns NN14 37 D7
Fletcher Rd NN10 33 C5
Fletton Way PE8 31 B3
Flora Thompson Dr
NN13 12 A3
Flore Hill NN9 39 C2
Florence Rd NN1 29 G3

Flying Dutchman Way
NN11 18 B4
Folly Rd MK19 15 A5
Ford Dr NN13 12 A3
Ford St NN16 25 E5
Forest Ct NN13 13 F2
Forest Ct NN10 33 F5
Forest Gate Rd NN17 14 C1
Forest Glade NN16 24 E1
Forfar St NN5 28 A3
Forge Ho*,
High St NN14 35 B5
Forrester Dr NN13 12 B2
Forrester Gro NN14 37 D7
Fort Pl NN1 28 C4
Foskett Cl NN10 33 C5
Fosse Grn NN10 33 E5
Foster Cl NN15 25 B7
Foster Ct NN16 24 C5
Fotheringhay Ct NN14 37 E6
Fotheringhay Mews PE8 31 A1
Foundry Pl NN11 19 D5
Foundry St NN1 28 D5
Foundry Walk NN14 37 C7
Fourth Av NN8 40 B5
Fowey Cl NN8 40 A2
Fox Covert Dr NN7 35 D2
Fox La NN13 12 B5
Fox St NN14 35 B5
Foxglove Cl NN10 33 E8
Foxholes Cl MK19 15 B5
Foxlands NN14 17 D4
Foxton Cl NN15 25 C7
Foxwood Cl NN10 33 A6
Francis Ct NN10 33 A5
Francis Dickins Cl NN29 16 C5
Francis St NN9 34 A4
Francis Ter NN9 34 A4
Franciscan Cl NN10 33 B7
Franklin Flds NN17 14 E1
Franklin St NN5 28 A3
Franklin Way NN11 18 C2
Fraser Ct NN11 19 E5
Freehold St NN2 28 D1
Freeman Way NN9 16 D2
Freesch St NN1 28 C4
Friars Cl NN8 41 E4
Friary Cl NN11 19 D5
Frinton Cl NN10 33 B7
Frobisher Cl NN11 19 F5
Frog Hall NN12 36 B2
Fuller Rd NN3 27 A6
Fuller St NN16 25 F5
Furlong Rd NN14 17 E3
Furnace Dr,
Daventry NN11 18 B3
Furnace Dr,
Kettering NN16 37 C7
Furnace La,
Kettering NN16 24 B3
Furnace La,
Northampton NN7 30 A2
Furnells Cl NN9 34 C2
Fusilier Cl NN11 19 C5
Fusilier Way NN7 39 A3

Gable Ct NN11 19 B6
Gainsborough Ct NN18 14 B3
Gainsborough Dr NN8 40 D1
Gainsborough St NN18 14 A4
Gainsborough Way
NN11 18 D1
Ganton Cl NN11 18 F4
Garden Fields Cl NN9 22 D1
Garden Fields Cl NN29 23 D2
Gardenfield NN10 32 D3
Gardner Cl NN9 34 B2
Gardner Rise NN13 12 A4
Garfield St NN15 25 D7
Garners Way NN7 21 B1
Garrard Way NN16 24 B4
Garrick Rd NN1 29 H2
Garrow Cl NN9 22 A3
Gas St NN1 28 C4
Gates Cl NN9 22 A3
Gentian Cl NN10 33 E8
George Blackhall Ct*,
Rowley Rd NN17 14 A1
George Row NN1 28 D4
George St,
Burton Latimer NN15 13 F2
George St, Corby NN17 14 B2
George St,
Higham Ferrers NN10 32 E1
George St,
Irthlingborough NN9 22 A5
George St,
Kettering NN16 25 D6
George St,
Rushden NN10 33 D6
George St,
Wellingborough NN8 41 E2
Georges Av NN7 30 F4
Georges Ct NN7 30 F4
Gharana Nivas NN8 41 F2
Gibbons Dr NN14 35 D5
Gibson La NN5 28 A2
Gilbert Scott Cl NN12 38 B4
Gilchrist Av NN11 14 E1
Gillingham Rd NN15 25 B7

Gillitts Rd NN8 40 C4
Gipsy La,
Kettering NN16 24 A4
Gipsy La,
Wellingborough NN29 23 A2
Gisburne Rd NN8 41 F2
Glade Cl NN15 13 E2
Gladstone Rd NN5 28 B1
Gladstone St,
Desborough NN14 17 C2
Gladstone St,
Kettering NN16 25 E5
Gladstone St,
Rothwell NN14 35 B4
Gladstone Ter NN9 34 C3
Glaister Rd NN10 32 E1
Glamis Cl NN10 33 F7
Glapthorn Rd PE8 31 A1
Glasgow St NN5 28 A3
Glassbrook Rd NN10 33 B6
Glassthorpe La NN7 21 A2
Glebe Av NN15 25 D7
Glebe Dr NN13 12 D4
Glebe Rd,
Kettering NN16 13 C2
Glebe Rd,
Milton Keynes MK19 15 A4
Glebe Rise OX17 25 D7
Glebeland Av NN5 28 A1
Glebeland Gdns NN5 28 A1
Glebeland Rd NN5 28 A1
Glebeland Walk NN5 28 A1
Glen Bank NN8 41 F3
Glendon Rd NN14 35 C5
Glendower Cl NN11 18 B3
Gleneagles Cl NN11 18 F4
Gleneagles Dr NN8 40 B1
Glenfield Cl NN10 33 B5
Glenmore Cl NN10 24 D1
Gloucester Cl,
Kettering NN16 25 E5
Gloucester Cl,
Weedon NN7 39 B2
Gloucester Cres NN10 33 E5
Gloucester Ct NN14 35 B5
Gloucester Pl NN8 41 E3
Glovers La OX17 27 B2
Goadbys Yd*,
Church Walk NN16 25 D6
Godwin Cl NN13 12 B5
Gold End NN16 25 C5
Gold St,
Desborough NN14 17 C2
Gold St, Kettering NN16 25 D5
Gold St,
Northampton NN1 28 D4
Gold St,
Wellingborough NN8 41 E2
Goldcrest Rd NN13 12 A2
Golding Cl NN11 19 D5
Goldsmith Rd NN8 40 A3
Goodhew Cl NN15 25 B7
Goodwood Rd NN10 33 F8
Goose Grn NN13 12 A2
Goosemere MK19 15 B5
Gordon Rd,
Peterborough PE8 31 C2
Gordon Rd,
Wellingborough NN8 41 F2
Gordon St,
Kettering NN16 25 E5
Gordon St,
Northampton NN2 28 C2
Gordon St,
Rothwell NN14 35 B5
Gorseholm Ct NN9 22 B4
Gosforth Cl NN8 40 B4
Grace Cl NN15 13 D4
Grafton Cl NN8 40 B1
Grafton Rd,
Northampton NN7 35 B2
Grafton St,
Rushden NN10 33 F6
Grafton St,
Kettering NN16 24 C4
Grafton St,
Northampton NN1 28 C3
Graham Hill NN12 36 B3
Graham Hill Rd NN12 38 A2
Granby Cl NN29 16 B6
Grange Rd,
Northampton NN1 20 B2
Grange Cl,
Wellingborough NN29 23 C3
Grange Rd,
Kettering NN16 37 A7
Grange Rd,
Thrapston NN16 24 C4
Grangeway NN10 33 C7
Grant Cl NN15 25 B7
Grant Rd NN8 41 F3
Granville St NN16 25 E5
Grasmere Grn NN8 40 A4
Grasmere Rd NN16 25 B6
Grasmere Way NN10 33 A6
Grasscroft NN6 23 A5

Gravely St NN10 33 B6
Gray Cl NN6 20 C3
Gray St,
Northampton NN1 29 E2
Gray St,
Wellingborough NN29 23 B3
Grays Cl NN17 14 C1
Great La NN7 30 D4
Great Park St NN8 41 E3
Great Russell St NN1 29 E3
Grebe Cl NN14 37 D6
Green Cl NN8 40 B1
Green La,
Kettering NN16 25 D5
Green La,
Silverstone NN12 36 B3
Green La,
Thrapston NN14 37 C6
Green La,
Towcester NN12 38 A5
Green La,
Wellingborough NN9 34 C6
Green St,
Northampton NN1 28 C4
Green St,
Wellingborough NN29 16 C6
Greenacre Dr NN10 33 D8
Greenfield Av NN15 25 C7
Greenfield Way NN10 33 C7
Greenhill Cres NN11 18 C4
Greenhill Ct NN16 23 B5
Greenhill Rd,
Kettering NN15 25 B7
Greenhill Rd,
Northampton NN6 23 A5
Greening Rd NN14 35 A4
Greenland Cl NN8 40 A3
Greenslade Cl NN15 25 C7
Greenview Dr NN12 38 A4
Greenwood Rd NN5 28 B3
Gregory St NN1 28 C4
Gregory Walk NN14 14 B4
Grenadier Rd NN11 19 B5
Grendon Rd NN6 20 A5
Grenville Cl,
Daventry NN11 19 F6
Grenville Cl,
Kettering NN14 35 C5
Gresley Cl NN11 18 B3
Greyfriars NN1 28 C4
Greyfriars Rd NN11 19 C7
Griffith St NN10 33 D7
Grindleford Cl NN14 17 A2
Grizedale Cl NN16 24 C1
Grombold Av NN8 34 B3
Grosvenor Pl NN13 12 B4
Grosvenor Shopping
Centre NN1 28 D4
Grove Farm Cl NN16 23 D4
Grove Farm La NN3 27 B4
Grove Pl NN9 34 B4
Grove Rd,
Kettering NN14 37 C7
Grove Rd,
Northampton NN1 29 E3
Grove St Rushden NN10 33 E6
Grove St, Rushden NN9 34 B4
Grove St,
Wellingborough NN8 40 D2
Grove Way NN9 16 A3
Grovelands NN11 19 B6
Guildhall Rd NN1 28 D4
Guillemot La NN8 41 E1
Gunnell Cl NN15 25 B7

H.E. Bates Way NN10 33 C6
Hachenburg Pl NN10 32 E3
Hackwood Rd NN11 19 F7
Haddon Cl NN10 33 C7
Hadleigh Ho*,
Rectory Cl NN10 33 D6
Hadrians Gate NN13 12 D4
Haines Rd NN4 28 D6
Halfmoon Mews PE8 31 C3
Halford St NN14 37 C7
Hall Av NN10 33 C7
Hall Cl, Harpole NN7 21 B2
Hall Cl, Kettering NN15 25 B7
Hall Cl, Kislingbury NN7 21 D4
Hall Cl, Rugby CV23 26 C2
Hall Dr,
Northampton NN6 23 C5
Hall Rd,
Wellingborough NN9 16 B3
Halls La NN15 25 B6
Halls La NN13 12 B5
Hallwood Rd NN16 24 D3
Halse Rd NN13 12 B1
Hamblin Cl NN10 33 B6
Hamilton Ct*,
Elizabeth St NN17 14 C3
Hamlet Grn NN5 28 A2
Hammas Leys NN6 23 C5
Hampden Cres*,
Windmill Av NN15 25 F6
Hampton Court Cl NN12 38 B5
Hampton Dr OX17 26 B5
Hampton St NN1 28 C2

Handcross Way NN10 32 E4
Hanover Dr NN13 12 B3
Hans Apel Dr NN13 12 A4
Harbidges La NN6 23 B5
Harborough Rd, Kettering NN14 17 B1
Harborough Rd, Rushden NN10 33 E7
Harborough Way NN10 33 E4
Harcourt Mews NN6 20 B3
Harcourt Sq NN6 20 B3
Harcourt St, Kettering NN16 25 E5
Harcourt St, Wellingborough NN9 34 C3
Harding Ter NN1 28 C2
Hardwick Cl NN8 40 D3
Hardwick Rd NN8 40 B2
Haresmoor Dr NN12 38 C6
Harlech Ct NN14 37 E7
Harlestone Rd NN8 28 A2
Harmans Way NN7 39 B2
Harold St NN1 29 E4
Harrington Rd, Desborough NN14 17 A3
Harrington Rd, Rothwell NN14 35 A6
Harris Cl, Brackley NN13 12 A3
Harris Cl, Wellingborough NN8 34 C2
Harrison Cl NN8 40 C3
Harrison Ct NN14 30 E4
Harrow La NN11 18 E1
Harrowden Rd, Finedon NN9 16 A3
Harrowden Rd, Wellingborough NN8 40 D1
Harrowick La NN6 20 A3
Harry Cl NN6 23 B5
Hartwell Rd NN7 35 C2
Hartwood Cft NN16 24 F1
Harvest Cl, Daventry NN11 18 E1
Harvest Cl, Kettering NN15 13 E3
Harvey Cl NN9 34 A4
Harvey La NN3 27 A6
Harvey Rd, Rushden NN10 33 D8
Harvey Rd, Wellingborough NN8 40 C4
Harvey Reeves Rd NN5 28 A5
Harwood Dr NN16 24 C2
Hatton Av NN8 40 D2
Hatton Ct NN8 40 D2
Hatton Gdns NN8 40 D2
Hatton Park Rd NN8 40 D3
Hatton St NN8 40 D2
Havelock St, Desborough NN14 17 C2
Havelock St, Kettering NN16 24 D4
Havelock St, Wellingborough NN8 41 E3
Haven Cl NN5 28 B2
Haweswater Rd NN16 24 A4
Hawke Rd NN11 19 F6
Hawkins Cl, Brackley NN13 12 A4
Hawkins Cl, Daventry NN11 18 F4
Hawkins Cl, Kettering NN14 35 C5
Hawkshead Rd NN 40 A4
Hawson Cl NN15 25 E8
Hawthorn Cl NN15 13 D4
Hawthorn Dr, Brackley NN13 12 C2
Hawthorn Dr, Daventry NN11 18 C3
Hawthorn Dr, Kettering NN14 37 C8
Hawthorn Dr, Towcester NN12 38 C2
Hawthorn Rd, Burton Latimer NN15 13 D4
Hawthorn Rd, Kettering NN15 25 D7
Hawthorn Way NN8 40 C3
Hawthorne Rd NN9 16 C2
Hay Cl NN10 33 E8
Hay La NN9 16 C2
Hayden Av NN9 16 C2
Hayden Rd NN10 33 E6
Hayden Walk NN10 33 F6
Hayes Rd MK19 15 B4
Hayman Rd NN13 12 A4
Haynes Rd NN16 25 F5
Hayway, Rushden NN10 32 C4
Hayway, Wellingborough NN9 22 A5
Hazel Cl NN13 12 C2
Hazel Cres NN12 38 A5
Hazel Rd NN15 25 F6
Hazelden Cl NN29 16 B6
Hazelwood Rd, Corby NN17 14 C1
Hazelwood Rd, Northampton NN1 29 E4

Headingley Rd NN10 33 F6
Headlands, Desborough NN14 17 E2
Headlands, Kettering NN15 25 D8
Hearnden Ct NN8 40 C5
Heath Cote Gro NN14 17 A2
Heath Rise NN8 40 B1
Heath Ter NN12 38 B3
Heath Way NN15 13 E2
Heather Ct NN10 33 C6
Heatherbreea Gdns NN10 33 B5
Heathersage Cl NN14 17 A2
Heathfield Way NN5 28 B1
Heathville NN5 28 A1
Hecham Way NN10 32 D1
Hedgerow Way NN11 18 D1
Hemans Rd NN11 18 C3
Hembury Pl NN4 28 A6
Hemery Way NN15 25 B7
Hemmingwell Lodge Way NN8 41 F1
Hemmingwell Rd NN8 41 E1
Henley Cl NN8 40 B1
Henry Bird Ct NN4 28 D6
Henry Bird Way NN4 28 D6
Henry Smith Ho*, Queens Rd NN11 18 C4
Henry St NN1 29 F2
Henshaw Rd NN8 40 C5
Henson Cl NN16 24 B3
Henson Way NN16 24 A3
Herbert Gdns NN12 38 C1
Herbert Ho NN1 28 C3
Herbert St NN1 28 C3
Hereford Cl NN14 17 E2
Heritage Way NN14 34 C2
Herne Rd PE8 31 C4
Heron Av NN14 37 D6
Heron Cl, Kettering NN15 13 B3
Heron Cl, Towcester NN12 38 C6
Heron Ct NN11 18 D4
Heron Dr NN13 12 A2
Heron Way NN8 41 F1
Herrietts Farm Rd NN13 12 B3
Herriotts La NN8 41 E3
Hertford Ct NN11 19 D7
Hervey St NN1 29 E3
Hesketh Cres NN14 38 C5
Hesperus NN8 40 A3
Hester St NN2 28 D2
Hever Cl, Kettering NN14 37 E6
Hever Cl, Rushden NN10 33 F8
Heyford Rd NN7 30 B2
Hiawatha NN8 40 A3
Hickmire NN29 16 B4
Hicks Ct NN12 38 C5
Hicks Rd NN12 38 C5
Hidcote Cl NN8 40 B6
Hidcote Way NN11 18 B1
High Hill Av NN14 35 B5
High March NN11 19 E7
High March Cl NN11 19 F7
High St, Brackley NN13 12 C4
High St, Bugbrooke NN7 30 E3
High St, Burton Latimer NN15 13 E3
High St, Corby NN17 14 E2
High St, Crick NN6 15 C2
High St, Daventry NN11 19 D5
High St, Deanshanger MK19 15 A5
High St, Desborough NN14 17 C3
High St, Earls Barton NN6 20 B3
High St, Finedon NN9 16 B2
High St, Flore NN7 30 B2
High St, Harpole NN7 21 B2
High St, Higham Ferrers NN10 32 E3
High St, Irchester NN29 23 F2
High St, Irthlingborough NN9 22 A5
High St, Islip NN14 37 B6
High St, Kettering NN16 25 D6
High St, Kislingbury NN7 21 C4
High St, Long Buckby NN6 23 B4
High St, Middleton Cheney OX17 27 C2
High St, Moulton NN3 27 B5
High St, Raunds NN9 34 C3
High St, Roade NN7 35 B2
High St, Rothwell NN14 35 B5
High St, Rushden NN10 33 D5
High St, Silverstone NN12 36 B2
High St, Stanwick NN9 34 C3
High St, Thrapston NN14 37 C7
High St, Weedon NN7 39 B2
High St, Wellingborough NN8 40 D3
High St, Wollaston NN29 16 B5

High St South NN10 33 D7
High Stack NN6 23 C5
High Street Pl NN8 41 E3
High Vw MK19 15 A4
Higham Rd, Irchester NN8 23 A1
Higham Rd, Kettering NN15 13 E3
Higham Rd, Rushden NN10 32 D4
Higham Rd, Stanwick NN9 34 C6
Highfield Cl NN13 12 B5
Highfield Gro NN17 14 D1
Highfield Rd, Daventry NN11 18 B4
Highfield Rd, Irthlingborough NN9 22 B4
Highfield Rd, Kettering NN14 37 D7
Highfield Rd, Rushden NN10 33 B7
Highfield Rd, Thrapston NN15 25 D8
Highfield Rd, Wellingborough NN8 40 D4
Highfield St NN9 16 D2
Highfields NN12 38 B6
Highgrove Ct NN10 33 D6
Highlands Dr NN11 18 C2
Hill House Gdns NN9 34 C6
Hill St, Brackley NN13 12 B4
Hill St, Kettering NN16 24 C4
Hill St, Raunds NN9 34 C3
Hill St, Wellingborough NN8 40 D4
Hillary Cl NN11 18 C2
Hillary Rd NN10 33 C7
Hillcrest Av, Burton Latimer NN15 13 F4
Hillcrest Av, Kettering NN15 25 F6
Hillcrest Cl NN14 37 D6
Hillcrest Ct NN14 12 B4
Hillfield Rd PE8 31 A2
Hillside Av NN11 18 F4
Hillside Av, Towcester NN12 36 B1
Hillside Cres NN7 30 B2
Hillside Rd, Flore NN7 39 D1
Hillside Rd, Nether Heyford NN7 30 A2
Hillside Rd, Wellingborough NN8 41 G1
Hillstone Cl NN9 34 D6
Hilltop Av NN14 17 B2
Hilltop Cl NN14 17 B2
Hind Stile NN10 32 E3
Hinton Rd NN13 12 A5
Hinwick Rd NN29 16 B6
Hobbs Hill*, Kettering Rd NN14 35 B5
Hodge Way NN16 25 F5
Hodges La NN7 21 C4
Hoe Way NN7 35 A2
Hogarth Walk NN14 14 C3
Holbush Way NN9 22 A3
Holden Gro NN11 19 C5
Holdgate Cl NN13 12 B2
Holland Rise OX17 26 B6
Hollands Dr NN15 13 E3
Hollington Rd NN3 34 D3
Hollowell Ct NN8 40 D4
Holly Cl NN13 12 C2
Holly Ct, Kettering NN16 24 F3
Holly Rd, Northampton NN1 29 F2
Holly Rd, Rushden NN10 33 A5
Holly Walk NN9 16 A5
Hollyhill NN12 38 B5
Holme Cl NN7 39 A4
Holmes Av NN9 34 D3
Holmfield Dr NN9 34 D3
Holmfield Ter NN6 23 A4
Holyoake Rd NN29 16 B5
Holyoake Ter NN6 23 A4
Holyrood Rd NN5 28 A3
Home Cl, Banbury OX17 27 D3
Home Cl, Silverstone NN12 36 B2
Home Cl, Towcester NN12 38 B4
Home Cl, Wellingborough NN9 22 A6
Homefield NN16 19 C6
Homestead Cl NN3 27 C5
Homestead Dr NN7 35 C4
Homestead Way NN2 29 E1
Honey Hill Dr MK19 15 B5
Honeystones NN18 27 B5
Honiton Gdns NN18 14 A4
Hood Rd NN11 19 F5
Hood St NN1 29 E2
Hood Walk NN15 25 F7
Hookhams Path NN25 16 B6
Hopper Walk NN18 14 B3
Hopton Cl NN11 18 D1
Hornbeam Cl NN8 40 C3

Hornbeam Ct NN14 17 F3
Hornby Rd NN6 20 D2
Horncastle Cl NN11 18 D1
Horrell Ct NN10 33 D6
Horse Mkt, Kettering NN16 25 D5
Horse Mkt, Northampton NN1 28 D4
Horseshoe St NN1 28 D4
Horsley Rd NN2 28 C1
Horton Cl OX17 27 C3
Horton Cres OX17 27 C3
Horton Dr OX17 27 C3
Horton Rd OX17 27 C3
Hortons La NN14 37 D7
Hospital Hill*, Market Hill NN14 35 C5
Hove Rd NN10 33 E6
Howard Cl NN11 18 B4
Howard Ct NN8 41 F3
Howard Rd NN16 16 B6
Howard's Ct NN29 16 B6
Howden Grn NN14 17 A2
Howe Cres NN14 19 F6
Hudson Cl NN11 18 C2
Hulme Way NN8 40 C1
Humber Cl NN11 18 A3
Humber Gdns NN8 40 A1
Humphries Dr NN13 12 A3
Hunsbarrow Rd NN4 28 A6
Hunt Cl NN12 38 C2
Hunt St NN18 14 B3
Hunter St NN1 29 E3
Huntingdon Rd NN14 37 D7
Hurst Cl NN15 13 E1
Hussar Cl NN15 19 C5
Huxloe Pl NN16 25 D5
Hyde Cl NN7 35 B1
Hyde Rd NN7 35 A2

Imperial Ct NN10 33 D6
Independent St CV23 26 B2
Inkerman Way PE8 31 B3
Inlands Cl NN15 19 E5
Inlands Rise NN11 19 D6
Irchester Rd, Rushden NN10 33 A6
Irchester Rd, Wellingborough NN29 16 C5
Iron Duke Cl NN11 18 C3
Ironstone Ct NN9 16 B2
Irthlingborough Rd, Finedon NN9 16 C2
Irthlingborough Rd, Wellingborough NN8 41 F4
Irvine Dr NN12 38 C1
Ise Rd NN15 25 F6
Ise Vale Av NN14 17 E3
Ise View Rd NN14 17 D3
Isebrook Ct NN15 13 C3
Islington Ct*, Islington Rd NN12 38 C4
Islington Rd NN12 38 C4
Ivy Ct NN11 19 C6
Ivy La NN9 16 B3
Ivy Rd, Kettering NN16 24 F3
Ivy Rd, Northampton NN1 29 F2

Jacklin Ct NN8 40 B1
Jackson Way NN15 25 B7
Jacksons La NN8 40 D3
James Cl OX17 27 C2
James Rd NN8 41 E6
James St NN29 23 C3
James Watt Cl NN11 18 A3
Jarvis Cl NN13 12 C3
Jasmine Cl NN16 24 F3
Jasmine Rd NN16 24 F3
Jellicoe Cl NN11 19 F6
Jenkinson Rd NN12 38 D5
Jennings Cl, Daventry NN11 19 E6
Jennings Cl, Rushden NN10 32 D3
Jersey Cl NN8 41 F1
Jervis Cl NN11 19 E6
Jeyes Cl NN3 27 A5
Joan Pyel Cl NN9 16 C2
Jobs Yd NN16 25 D5
John Clare Cl NN13 12 C1
John Clare Ct NN16 24 E2
John Eagle Cl NN8 34 C6
John Pyel Rd NN9 22 A5
John Smith Av NN14 35 D5
John St, Kettering NN14 37 D6
John St, Rushden NN10 33 D6
Johns Rd NN7 30 F3
Johnson Av NN13 12 A3
Johnson Cl NN11 18 C4
Jonathon Ct NN13 12 D6
Jones Cl NN13 12 A4
Jubilee Av NN14 14 A4
Jubilee Av NN14 37 A5
Jubilee Cres NN8 40 D6
Jubilee Cl NN9 16 C2
Jubilee Rd NN11 19 C5
Jubilee St, Kettering NN14 35 B6

Jubilee St, Wellingborough NN9 22
Jubilee Ter NN14 13
Juniper Cl NN12 38
Jutland Way NN16

Keats Cl NN6
Keats Dr, Kettering NN16 2
Keats Dr, Towcester NN12 3
Keats Rd, Daventry NN11 1
Keats Rd, Wellingborough NN8 4
Keats Way, Corby NN17 14
Keats Way, Higham Ferrers NN10 32
Keats Way, Rushden NN10 3
Keble Cl NN11 19
Keble Cl NN13 12
Kelmarsh Rd NN17 1
Kelvin Gro NN17 1
Kendal Cl, Rushden NN10 3
Kendal Cl, Wellingborough NN8 4
Kenilworth Cl, Daventry NN11 1
Kenilworth Cl, Kettering Gdns NN14
Kenmore Dr NN14 17
Kenmuir Rd NN9 1
Kennedy Cl NN11 1
Kennet Cl NN8 4
Kensington Cl, Banbury OX17 2
Kensington Cl, Rushden NN10 3
Kensington Cl, Towcester NN12 3
Kensington Gdns NN15 2
Kent Cl NN17 1
Kent Rd NN10 3
Keston Way NN9 3
Kestrel Cres NN13 1
Keswick NN8
Kettering Gdns*, Abington Sq NN1
Kettering Rd, Burton Latimer NN15 1
Kettering Rd, Isham NN15 1
Kettering Rd, Kettering NN14
Kettering Rd, Moulton NN3
Kettering Rd, Northampton NN1
Kettering Rd, Rothwell NN14 3
Kettonby Gdns NN15 2
Kilborn Cl NN8 4
Kilborn Rd NN8 4
Kilburn Pl NN10 3
Kilby Cl NN8 4
Kilnway NN8 4
Kimbolton Ct NN14
Kimbolton Rd NN10 3
King Edward Rd NN1 2
King St, Desborough NN14 1
King St, Kettering NN16 1
King St, New Barton NN6
King St, Northampton NN1
King Style Cl NN6 1
Kingfisher Rd NN11 1
Kingfisher Way NN15 1
Kings Av NN10 3
Kings Ct NN14 1
Kings Grn NN11 1
Kings La NN7
Kings Meadow La NN10 3
Kings Pk NN7 3
Kings Pl NN10 3
Kings Rd, Peterborough PE8 3
Kings Rd, Rushden NN10 3
Kings St NN8 4
Kings Stile OX17 2
Kingsfield Cl NN5 2
Kingsfield Way NN5 2
Kingshill Dr MK19 1
Kingsley Av, Daventry NN11 1
Kingsley Av, Kettering NN16
Kingsley Ct*, Kingsley Rd NN14 1
Kingsley Gdns NN2
Kingsley Rd, Kettering NN14 3
Kingsley Rd, Northampton NN2
Kingsley Rd, Towcester NN12 3

gsmith Dr NN9 — 34 D3
gsthorpe Rd NN2 — 28 D1
gston Cl, nbury OX17 — 27 D3
gston Cl, venty NN11 — 18 C4
gston Cl, rthampton NN6 — 23 C5
gsway NN8 — 40 C5
swell St NN1 — 28 D4
ing Dr NN12 — 38 B4
ing Rd, Corby NN17 — 14 A1
ettering NN16 — 24 E2
ton Cl NN4 — 35 C5
ton Fld NN14 — 35 D5
ingbury Rd NN7 — 30 E3
apdale Cl NN16 — 24 C1
phill Cres NN4 — 28 C2
ghtlands Rd NN9 — 22 B3
ghtley Rd NN7 — 28 C1
ghts Cl NN6 — 20 B3
ghts Cl NN10 — 41 E2
wles Cl NN10 — 33 F5
x Ct NN8 — 41 F3
x Mews NN8 — 41 F3
x Rd NN8 — 41 F3
uston Dr NN10 — 33 B6
utsford La NN6 — 23 C4
nesworth Gdns N10 — 32 E2

urnum Cl NN8 — 40 C3
urnum Cres NN16 — 24 F3
dermakers Yd NN7 — 30 D3
ybower Cl NN16 — 24 A4
ycroft NN15 — 19 C5
ys La NN1 — 28 D3
e Av NN15 — 28 D3
e Cres NN11 — 19 B5
eside Ct NN14 — 37 D6
nport Dr NN11 — 18 B2
caster Cl NN29 — 16 B4
caster Dr, ackley NN13 — 12 B3
caster Dr, ettering NN14 — 37 E6
caster Rd, ttering NN16 — 24 E4
caster Rd, othwell NN14 — 35 C5
caster St NN10 — 32 E2
caster Way NN10 — 33 F5
cers Way NN7 — 39 B3
chester Way NN11 — 18 A4
cum Ho NN8 — 40 C3
dor NN8 — 40 B3
dseer Ct NN18 — 14 B3
gdale NN14 — 17 B2
gdale Ct NN8 — 40 B2
gdale Gro NN17 — 14 B1
gdon Cl NN11 — 18 B2
gham Rd NN9 — 34 B2
gley Cres NN9 — 22 D1
gley Ct NN15 — 13 D3
gsett Cl NN16 — 24 A4
gton Pl NN14 — 13 A4
sdown Cl NN11 — 18 D2
som Cl NN15 — 13 F2
ford Rd NN8 — 14 C4
ch Cl NN29 — 23 B3
ch Dr NN11 — 18 D2
chwood Cl NN8 — 40 C3
k Rise NN13 — 12 B3
khall La NN7 — 21 B1
khall Way NN7 — 12 C1
khill NN10 — 32 D4
kin Gdns NN10 — 32 C3
kwood Cl NN16 — 24 E1
ham Rd PE8 — 31 B2
nbury Rd NN13 — 12 A3
imer Pk
imer Cl NN15
d Est NN15 — 13 C1
ymer Ct NN1 — 28 D3
da Way NN12 — 38 C1
ds Rd NN6 — 15 C3
reate Ho NN8 — 18 C3
rel Ct NN8 — 41 F3
rel Pl NN12 — 38 C4
rel Rd NN6 — 24 E4
ender Ct NN14 — 37 D6
ender Way NN10 — 33 E8
ery Ct NN18 — 14 B3
vrence Ct, orby NN18 — 14 B3
vrence Ct, ong Buckby NN6 — 23 B4
vrence Ct, rthampton NN1 — 28 D2
vs Cft NN13 — 12 A4
vs La NN9 — 16 B2
vson St, ttering NN16 — 24 E4
vson St, ellingborough NN9 — 34 C3
vton Rd NN9 — 33 E5
ton Dr PE8 — 31 D2

Laywood Cl NN9 — 34 B2
Laywood Way NN9 — 22 A6
Lea Rd NN1 — 29 G2
Lea Way NN8 — 40 B4
Leamington Way NN11 — 19 A6
Leatherland Ct*, Carrington St NN16 — 25 D5
Lee Way NN9 — 34 B2
Lees St NN9 — 22 A5
Leeson Cl NN12 — 38 C5
Leeson Rd NN12 — 38 C5
Legion Cres NN16 — 24 B4
Leicester Cl NN16 — 24 C4
Leicester St, Kettering NN16 — 24 C4
Leicester St, Northampton NN1 — 28 D2
Leicester Ter NN2 — 28 D2
Leighton Pl NN8 — 41 E3
Leighton Rd NN18 — 14 B3
Lely Ct NN18 — 14 B3
Leonard La NN3 — 27 A5
Leonardo Ct*, Leighton Rd NN18 — 14 B3
Leslie Rd NN2 — 28 C2
Letts Rd NN4 — 28 C6
Levitts Rd NN7 — 30 E3
Lewin Cl NN14 — 35 A5
Lewis Rd, Kettering NN15 — 25 E8
Lewis Rd, Northampton NN5 — 28 A2
Lexton Gdns OX17 — 27 D2
Leyland Trading Est NN8 — 41 H4
Leyland Vw NN8 — 41 H4
Leys Av, Desborough NN14 — 17 E3
Leys Av, Rothwell NN14 — 35 B4
Leys Cl NN6 — 23 C4
Leys Gdns NN8 — 41 G2
Leys Rd, Northampton NN6 — 20 A3
Leys Rd, Wellingborough NN8 — 41 F2
Lichfield Cl NN11 — 21 D4
Lilac Cl NN14 — 37 D6
Lilac Ct NN8 — 40 C3
Lilac Pl NN15 — 25 F6
Lilford Rd NN16 — 25 F5
Lilley Ter NN9 — 22 B4
Lime Av, Long Buckby NN6 — 23 C4
Lime Av, Northampton NN3 — 29 H1
Lime Av, Peterborough PE8 — 31 B2
Lime Cl NN9 — 22 B4
Lime Gdns NN9 — 22 C4
Lime Gro, Northampton NN7 — 30 F3
Lime Gro, Wellingborough NN8 — 41 E1
Lime Rd NN16 — 24 E1
Lime St, Rushden NN10 — 32 D4
Lime St, Wellingborough NN9 — 22 B4
Lime Ter NN9 — 22 B4
Lime Trees Gro NN17 — 14 E2
Lincoln Cl NN13 — 12 C6
Lincoln Pk NN13 — 12 C6
Lincoln Rd NN5 — 28 B4
Lincoln Walk NN18 — 14 A4
Lincoln Way NN11 — 19 D7
Linden Av, Kettering NN16 — 25 F5
Linden Av, Rushden NN10 — 32 D2
Linden Cl NN15 — 25 F6
Lindisfarne Way NN14 — 37 E7
Lindrick Cl NN11 — 19 F5
Lindsay St NN16 — 24 D4
Link Rd NN10 — 33 D8
Link Way, Northampton NN7 — 30 F4
Link Way, Towcester NN12 — 38 B5
Linley Dr NN14 — 17 B2
Linnell Way NN16 — 24 B3
Linnet Rd NN18 — 38 B6
Linnetts La NN10 — 32 E3
Lister Rd NN8 — 41 E2
Litchfield Cl NN16 — 24 E1
Little Cross St NN1 — 28 C4
Little La NN29 — 16 B4
Little London, Milton Keynes MK19 — 15 A5
Little London, Towcester NN12 — 36 B1
Little Priel Rd NN7 — 39 B3
Little St NN10 — 33 E7
Little Wood Cl NN5 — 28 B2
Littledale NN8 — 40 B1
Littlek St NN8 — 41 E3
Littlewood St NN14 — 35 C4
Livingstone St NN14 — 35 D5
Livingstone Rd NN11 — 18 B3
Llewellyn Walk NN18 — 14 B3
Lloyds Rd NN17 — 14 E2
Loatland St NN14 — 17 B2
Lobelia Rd NN16 — 24 E3

Loddington Rd NN14 — 35 B6
Lodge Green Rd NN17 — 14 C1
Lodge Rd, Daventry NN11 — 19 D5
Lodge Rd, Rushden NN10 — 33 D8
Lodge Way NN11 — 32 A1
London End, Northampton NN6 — 20 A3
London End, Wellingborough NN29 — 23 C3
London Rd, Daventry NN11 — 19 D6
London Rd, Kettering NN16 — 25 D5
London Rd, Northampton NN4 — 28 D6
London Rd, Raunds NN9 — 34 A1
London Rd, Roade NN7 — 35 B2
London Rd, Towcester NN12 — 38 C4
London Rd, Wellingborough NN8 — 41 F4
London Rd, Wollaston NN8 — 16 A5
Long Acres Dr NN9 — 22 A3
Long March Ind Est NN11 — 19 E7
Long Wall NN13 — 12 B5
Longburges OX17 — 27 D3
Longcroft Rd NN17 — 14 E4
Longfellow Dr NN16 — 24 E1
Longfellow Rd NN8 — 40 A3
Lonsborough Dr NN15 — 25 B7
Lonsdale Rd NN15 — 25 D8
Lorne Ct NN17 — 14 C3
Lorne Rd NN1 — 28 D2
Losby Cl NN10 — 33 C8
Louise Rd NN1 — 33 F7
Louth Dr NN10 — 33 F7
Lovell Cl NN9 — 34 D5
Lovell Ct NN9 — 22 B4
Low March NN11 — 19 E7
Lower Adelaide St NN2 — 28 C2
Lower Bath St NN1 — 28 C3
Lower Harding St NN1 — 28 C3
Lower Hester St NN2 — 28 C2
Lower King St NN14 — 17 D3
Lower Mounts NN1 — 28 C3
Lower Priory St NN1 — 28 C3
Lower St, Desborough NN14 — 17 C3
Lower St, Kettering NN16 — 25 C5
Lower Stable Yd NN14 — 38 C4
Lower Steeping NN14 — 17 D4
Lower Thrift St NN1 — 29 F3
Lowick Rd NN14 — 37 A5
Loyd Rd NN1 — 29 G3
Lucas Cl NN9 — 22 A6
Lucas Rd NN6 — 23 B5
Lunchfield Ct NN3 — 27 B6
Lunchfield Gdns NN3 — 27 B6
Lunchfield La NN3 — 27 A6
Lunchfield Walk NN3 — 27 B6
Lundy Av NN18 — 14 C4
Lupin Cl NN10 — 24 F3
Lutterworth Rd NN1 — 29 G3
Lydia Cl NN10 — 33 C6
Lyle Ct NN8 — 40 A1
Lyncroft Way NN2 — 28 C1
Lynford Way NN10 — 33 B8
Lynmouth Pl NN18 — 14 C4
Lynton Gro NN18 — 14 C4
Lynwood Cl NN16 — 24 D2
Lytham Ct NN8 — 40 B1
Lyttleton Rd NN5 — 28 B3
Lyveden Pl NN16 — 24 E3

Mallard Cl, Northampton NN6 — 20 B1
Mallard Cl, Rushden NN10 — 32 E1
Mallard Dr NN15 — 13 C3
Mallery Cl NN10 — 33 F5
Mallory Way NN11 — 18 C2
Mallows Dr NN9 — 34 B1
Malt Mill CV23 — 26 C2
Malt Mill Cl CV23 — 26 C3
Malt Mill Grn CV23 — 26 C3
Malthouse Cl NN9 — 22 B4
Malthouse Ct NN14 — 38 C4
Malvern Cl NN16 — 24 D1
Manchester Rd NN29 — 16 B5
Manfield Rd NN1 — 29 G2
Manning St NN10 — 33 E7
Manningham Rd NN9 — 34 D5
Mannings Rise NN10 — 33 E8
Mannock Rd NN8 — 40 C5
Manor Cl, Bunbury OX17 — 27 D3
Manor Cl, Harpole NN7 — 21 B2
Manor Cl, Kettering NN14 — 13 B4
Manor Cl, Roade NN7 — 35 C2
Manor Cl, Thrapston NN14 — 37 D6
Manor Cl, Wellingborough NN29 — 23 D2
Manor Court Lodge Ct NN8 — 41 F3
Manor Ct, Brackley NN13 — 12 C3
Manor Ct, Rushden NN10 — 33 E7
Manor Dr NN9 — 22 C4
Manor Farm Rd NN9 — 34 C3
Manor Gdns NN9 — 34 D6
Manor House Cl NN6 — 20 B3
Manor House Gdns NN9 — 34 C2
Manor Pk NN7 — 30 A1
Manor Pl NN15 — 25 E8
Manor Rd, Brackley NN13 — 12 B5
Manor Rd, Daventry NN11 — 19 E6
Manor Rd, Moulton NN3 — 27 A6
Manor Rd, New Barton NN6 — 20 B2
Manor Rd, Rothwell NN14 — 35 A5
Manor Rd, Rugby CV23 — 26 B2
Manor Rd, Rushden NN10 — 33 D8
Manor Rd, Weedon NN7 — 39 B3
Manor St NN9 — 34 C2
Manor Walk NN7 — 30 A1
Manor Way NN10 — 32 E3
Mansell Cl NN12 — 38 C1
Mansfield Cl NN14 — 17 C2
Mansfield St NN9 — 34 C3
Mansion Hill OX17 — 27 B3
Manton Cl NN18 — 33 E6
Manton Rd, Rushden NN10 — 33 E6
Manton Rd, Wellingborough NN9 — 22 A4
Maple Cl, Brackley NN13 — 12 B1
Maple Cl, Northampton NN7 — 30 E4
Maple Dr NN8 — 40 C3
Maple Rd, Kettering NN16 — 24 F4
Maple Rd, Rushden NN10 — 33 E6
Maple Wood NN10 — 33 D8
Mapletoft St NN9 — 34 B4
Marfair NN1 — 28 C4
Margaret Av NN8 — 40 D6
Margaret St NN1 — 29 E3
Market Hill NN14 — 35 B5
Market Pl, Brackley NN13 — 12 B5
Market Pl, Kettering NN16 — 25 D6
Market Pl, Northampton NN1 — 23 B4
Market Pl, Peterborough PE8 — 31 C4
Market Rd NN14 — 37 C7
Market Sq, Daventry NN11 — 19 D5
Market Sq, Northampton NN1 — 28 D4
Market Sq, Rushden NN10 — 32 E3
Market St, Kettering NN16 — 25 D6
Market St, Northampton NN1 — 29 F3
Market St, Wellingborough NN8 — 41 E3
Market Street Mews*, Market St NN16 — 25 D6
Marks Cl NN9 — 34 D6
Marlborough Av NN8 — 40 C1

Marlborough Cft NN13 — 12 B5
Marlborough Cl OX17 — 26 B5
Marlborough Rd NN5 — 28 B4
Marlow Cl NN11 — 19 C6
Marlow Ho NN14 — 17 C3
Marlow Rd NN12 — 38 C5
Marriots Rd NN6 — 23 C5
Marriott Cl NN9 — 22 A6
Marriott St NN2 — 28 D2
Marsh Cl NN6 — 15 C2
Marsh La NN9 — 22 C4
Marshalls Ct NN9 — 34 B3
Marshalls Rd NN9 — 34 B2
Marsons Dr NN6 — 15 C3
Marston Way NN11 — 18 D2
Martial Daire Blvd NN13 — 12 B2
Martin Cl NN10 — 32 D4
Martin Rd NN15 — 25 E8
Martins Yd NN5 — 28 C3
Marvius Mill Rd NN4 — 28 C6
Masefield Cl NN8 — 40 A4
Masefield Dr NN10 — 33 A6
Masefield Rd NN16 — 24 E3
Mason Cl, Kettering NN14 — 37 D7
Mason Cl, Peterborough PE8 — 31 C4
Matlock Way NN14 — 17 A2
Matson Cl NN14 — 35 A5
Matson Ct NN9 — 34 D2
Maunsell Rise NN14 — 35 A5
May Bank NN11 — 19 C6
Mayfield Rd, Daventry NN11 — 18 C3
Mayfield Rd, Kettering NN16 — 17 E3
McGibbon Walk NN9 — 22 A6
Mcinnes Way NN9 — 34 B2
Mead Rd NN15 — 25 B7
Meadow Cl, Daventry NN11 — 18 E1
Meadow Cl, Rushden NN10 — 32 D2
Meadow Ct NN12 — 38 B4
Meadow Dr NN10 — 32 D2
Meadow Farm Cl NN7 — 39 F2
Meadow Rd, Kettering NN16 — 25 C6
Meadow Rd, Rothwell NN14 — 35 A5
Meadow Vw NN10 — 32 D2
Meadow Walk, Wellingborough NN9 — 22 B4
Meadow Way NN9 — 22 B5
Meadway NN7 — 30 E3
Medway Dr NN8 — 40 A2
Medwin Rd NN8 — 41 G3
Meeting La, Corby NN17 — 14 F2
Meeting La, Kettering NN15 — 13 E3
Meeting La, Rothwell NN14 — 35 B5
Meeting La, Towcester NN12 — 38 C4
Meeting La, Wellingborough NN9 — 22 B4
Meissen Av NN14 — 17 B3
Melbourne Rd NN8 — 28 A4
Melbourne St NN1 — 29 F3
Melbourne Walk*, South St NN1 — 29 F3
Melloway Rd NN10 — 33 A6
Melton Rd NN8 — 41 G3
Melton Road North NN8 — 41 F2
Melton St NN16 — 24 D4
Melville St NN1 — 29 F3
Memorial Grn NN7 — 35 C2
Mendip Cl NN16 — 24 D2
Mendip Ct NN11 — 18 C2
Mercers Row NN1 — 28 D4
Mercury Cl NN11 — 18 A3
Merefields NN9 — 22 A3
Merri Vale Cl NN15 — 25 B8
Merthyr Rd NN5 — 28 A2
Merton Cl NN13 — 12 A3
Merton Rd NN11 — 19 C7
Michaelmas Cl OX17 — 27 B1
Middle Grass NN11 — 22 A3
Middle March NN11 — 19 E7
Middle St, Kettering NN14 — 13 B4
Middle St, Northampton NN7 — 30 B1
Middle St, Rugby CV23 — 26 B2
Middle Way OX17 — 27 C2
Middlewich Cl NN11 — 18 D1
Midland Bsns Units NN8 — 41 G1
Midland Rd, Higham Ferrers NN10 — 32 E3
Midland Rd, Kettering NN14 — 37 C7
Midland Rd, Raunds NN9 — 34 C2
Midland Rd, Rushden NN10 — 33 C5
Midland Rd, Wellingborough NN8 — 41 E3

47

St Marys Way,
Roade NN7 35 B1
St Marys Way,
Weedon Bec NN7 39 B4
St Michaels Gdns NN15 25 E7
St Michael's La NN29 16 B5
St Michaels Rd,
Kettering NN15 25 D7
St Michaels Rd,
Northampton NN1 29 E3
St Michaels Av NN1 29 F2
St Michaels Mount NN1 29 F2
St Nicholas Way NN14 37 A5
St Osyths La PE8 31 C4
St Pauls Ct NN15 25 D6
St Pauls Rd NN2 25 D6
St Peter's Av NN16 33 B6
St Peter's Cl NN11 19 C7
St Peters Ct NN9 34 C2
St Peters Gate NN13 12 D4
St Peters Rd,
Brackley NN13 12 C3
St Peters Rd,
Peterborough PE8 31 B1
St Peters Sq NN1 28 D4
St Peters St NN1 28 C4
St Peters Way,
Corby NN17 14 E2
St Peters Way,
Northampton NN1 28 C4
St Peters Way,
Weedon Bec NN7 39 B4
St Peters Way,
Wellingborough NN9 22 B4
St Rumbolds Dr OX17 26 C6
St Wilfrids Rd PE8 31 B2
Salcey Cl NN11 18 C2
Salem Cl NN6 23 A5
Salem La NN8 41 E3
Salisbury Rd NN8 41 G3
Salisbury St,
Kettering NN16 24 E3
Salisbury St,
Northampton NN2 28 C2
Salmons La OX17 27 D3
Samuels Cl NN9 34 C6
Sandby Rd NN18 14 B4
Sanders Ter NN6 23 B4
Sanderson Cl NN15 25 C7
Sandhill Rd NN5 28 A3
Sandpiper Cl NN15 13 C3
Sandringham Cl,
Brackley NN13 12 B4
Sandringham Cl,
Northampton NN1 29 H3
Sandringham Cl,
Rushden NN10 33 C6
Sandringham Cl,
Towcester NN12 38 B5
Sandringham Cl,
Wellingborough NN8 40 C6
Sandringham Cl,
Banbury OX17 26 B5
Sandringham Rd,
Northampton NN1 29 H2
Sandy Cl NN8 40 D2
Sandy Hill La NN3 27 C5
Sandy La NN7 21 D3
Sandyhome Rd NN12 38 B5
Sapphire Cl NN16 25 E6
Sargent Rd NN18 14 C4
Sartoris Rd NN10 33 C6
Sassoon Cl NN8 40 A2
Sassoon Mews NN8 40 A2
Saunders Cl NN16 25 C6
Saxby Cres NN8 41 G4
Saxilby Cl NN18 14 A4
Saxon Acre NN13 12 B4
Saxon Cl,
Kettering NN14 17 C3
Saxon Cl,
Rushden NN10 32 D1
Saxon Dale NN16 24 E1
Saxon Rise,
Northampton NN6 20 B4
Saxon Rise,
Wellingborough NN29 23 D2
Saxon St NN3 29 H1
Saxon Way NN9 33 A5
Saxonlea Cl NN10 33 A5
Sayers Cl NN12 36 A3
Scarborough St NN9 22 A4
Scarletwell St NN1 28 C3
Scharpwell NN8 22 A3
Scholars Ct NN1 29 E4
School Hill NN29 23 C2
School La, Harpole NN7 21 A1
School La, Islip NN14 37 A6
School La,
Kettering NN16 25 D5
School La,
Kislingbury NN7 21 C4
School La,
Northampton NN3 27 B5
School La,
Rothwell NN14 35 B5
School La,
Rushden NN10 32 D1
School La,
Wellingborough NN29 23 C2
School Pl NN18 14 A4
School Rd NN29 23 C2
School St NN11 19 B5
Scotland St NN16 24 E4
Scotney Way NN14 37 E6
Scotsmere NN9 22 A3
Scott Av NN14 35 D4
Scott Cl NN11 18 D3
Scott Rd, Corby NN17 14 E3
Scott Rd, Kettering NN16 24 E2
Scott Rd,
Wellingborough NN8 40 B4
Scotter Walk NN18 14 A4
Scythe Rd NN11 18 D1
Seagrave St NN15 25 E7
Sears Cl NN7 39 E1
Seaton Cres NN18 14 C4
Second Av NN8 40 B5
Second La NN5 28 A4
Sedge Cl NN14 37 C7
Sedgemoor Ct NN11 18 C1
Sedgemoor Way NN11 18 C1
SelWayn Cl NN11 19 D7
Semilong Rd NN2 28 D2
Senna Dr NN12 38 C1
Senwick Dr NN8 41 G4
Senwick Rd NN8 41 G3
Serve Cl NN8 41 E6
Settlers Flds NN15 25 C8
Severn Cl NN8 40 A1
Severn St NN5 13 D3
Severn Way NN16 24 C3
Sexton Cl NN11 18 C4
Seymour Pl PE8 31 A2
Seymour St NN15 28 B3
Shackleton Cl NN14 35 D5
Shackleton Cl NN12 18 C2
Shaftesbury Ho NN8 41 E5
Shaftesbury St NN16 25 E5
Shakespeare Av NN11 19 C5
Shakespeare Dr NN15 13 C3
Shakespeare Rd,
Kettering NN16 24 D2
Shakespeare Rd,
Northampton NN1 29 E2
Shakespeare Rd,
Rushden NN10 33 A6
Shakespeare Rd,
Wellingborough NN8 40 A4
Shannon Cl NN10 33 F5
Shannon Way NN15 13 D3
Sharman Rd,
Northampton NN5 28 B4
Sharman Rd,
Wellingborough NN8 41 E4
Sharman Way NN14 35 D5
Sharpes La NN6 23 B4
Sharwood Ter NN29 23 C2
Sheaf St NN11 19 D5
Shearwater La NN8 41 F1
Sheep St,
Kettering NN16 25 D6
Sheep St,
Northampton NN1 28 D3
Sheep St,
Wellingborough NN8 41 E4
Sheffield Ct NN9 34 B4
Sheffield Way NN6 20 B4
Shelley Cl,
Daventry NN11 19 C5
Shelley Cl,
Towcester NN12 38 A5
Shelley Dr NN10 32 D3
Shelley Rd,
Kettering NN16 24 E2
Shelley Rd,
Wellingborough NN8 40 A4
Shelmerdine Rise NN9 34 C3
Shelton Cl NN29 16 B5
Shepherds Hill NN29 16 D6
Shepherds Walk,
Bugbrooke NN7 30 F3
Shepherds Walk,
Harpole NN7 21 C2
Sherborne Way NN14 37 E6
Sheriff Rd NN1 29 G2
Sherwood Dr NN11 18 C3
Ship La PE8 31 B4
Shires Rd NN13 12 D5
Shirley Rd NN10 33 D5
Shoemakers Ct NN10 33 D5
Short La NN8 40 D3
Short Stocks NN10 33 F5
Shortwoods Cl NN9 34 C4
Shurville Cl NN6 20 B4
Sibley Rd NN9 16 D2
Siddeley Way NN11 18 A4
Siddons Cl PE8 31 A2
Siddons Way NN14 27 C5
Sidmouth Walk NN18 14 D4
Silver Cl,
Kettering NN16 25 D5
Silver St,
Northampton NN1 28 D3
Silver St,
Wellingborough NN8 41 E3
Silver Wood Ct NN15 25 E7
Silverdale Gro NN10 33 A6

Silverstone Tech Pk
NN12 36 B5
Silverwood Rd NN15 25 E7
Simpson Av NN10 32 E1
Sinclair Dr NN8 40 A1
Sissinghurst Dr NN14 37 E6
Skegness Walk NN18 14 A4
Skin Yard La NN6 23 C5
Skinners Hill NN10 33 D6
Slade Cres NN15 25 D8
Slade Leas OX17 27 D2
Slade Valley Av NN15 35 D5
Slaters Cl NN10 33 F6
Smarts Cl NN13 12 A3
Smarts Est CV23 26 C2
Smith Ct NN9 34 B3
Smitherway NN7 30 F3
Smithfield Pl NN9 34 B3
Sollys Way NN12 38 B5
Somerford Rd NN8 40 C1
Somerset St NN1 29 E3
Somerville Rd,
Brackley NN13 12 A3
Somerville Rd,
Daventry NN11 19 C7
Sondes Cl PE8 31 A2
Sopwith Way NN11 18 B2
Sorrell Cl NN14 13 A4
Soudan Av NN13 12 B3
Sourton Pl NN11 18 B5
South Av NN15 13 D2
South Bridge Cl PE8 31 B4
South Cl,
Northampton NN6 23 B5
South Cl, Rushden NN10 33 E7
South March NN11 19 E7
South Pk NN10 33 D7
South Pl NN10 19 C5
South Rd, Corby NN17 14 E2
South Rd,
Peterborough PE8 31 B4
South St,
Kettering NN14 13 B4
South St,
Northampton NN1 29 F1
South St, Weedon NN7 39 C4
South St,
Wellingborough NN29 16 B5
South Ter NN1 29 G3
South Vw,
Kislingbury NN7 21 D3
South Vw,
Nether Heyford NN7 30 A2
South Vw,
Northampton NN7 35 C2
South Way NN11 19 E5
Southall Rd NN17 14 F2
Southfield Av NN4 28 D6
Southfield Dr NN15 13 B1
Southfields NN10 33 E7
Southfields Dr NN6 15 C3
Southgate Dr,
Kettering NN15 25 F5
Southgate Dr,
Towcester NN12 38 C4
Southlands NN15 25 D7
Southwood Ho NN8 41 E5
Sovereigns Ct NN16 24 E1
Sower Leys Rd NN18 14 A4
Sparke Cl NN8 40 C1
Speke Dr NN11 18 D2
Spencer Bridge Rd NN5 28 B3
Spencer Cl,
Bugbrooke NN7 30 F3
Spencer Cl,
Earls Barton NN6 20 C3
Spencer Ct, Corby NN17 14 C3
Spencer Ct,
Rushden NN10 33 C5
Spencer Gdns NN13 12 B5
Spencer Haven NN5 28 B2
Spencer Par,
Northampton NN1 29 E4
Spencer Par,
Northampton NN9 34 C6
Spencer Rd,
Long Buckby NN6 23 B5
Spencer Rd,
Northampton NN1 29 E3
Spencer Rd,
Rushden NN10 32 C4
Spencer Rd,
Wellingborough NN9 22 A5
Spencer St,
Burton Latimer NN15 13 D3
Spencer St,
Kettering NN16 24 D4
Spencer St,
Rothwell NN14 35 C4
Spencer St,
Wellingborough NN9 34 C3
Spencer Walk NN9 34 C3
Spenser Cres NN11 18 B4
Spey Cl NN8 40 D1
Spiers Dr NN13 12 A4
Spilsby Rd NN18 14 A4
Spinney Cl,
Kettering NN14 37 D8

Spinney Cl,
Rushden NN10 33 B6
Spinney Cl,
Towcester NN11 38 B6
Spinney Dr NN15 25 F8
Spinney Gro NN17 14 C1
Spinney La NN15 25 F8
Spinney Rd,
Kettering NN15 13 E2
Spinney Rd,
Rushden NN10 33 B6
Spinney Rd,
Wellingborough NN9 22 B4
Spinney Rise NN11 19 D6
Spinney St NN9 34 B3
Spinney Ter NN9 22 B4
Sponnes Rd NN12 38 C5
Spring Cl, Brackley NN13 12 C4
Spring Cl,
Daventry NN11 19 D6
Spring Cl, Rugby CV23 26 B3
Spring Cl,
Wellingborough NN9 22 B4
Spring Gdns,
Daventry NN11 19 C6
Spring Gdns,
Earls Barton NN6 20 B3
Spring Gdns,
Kettering NN15 13 E2
Spring Gdns,
Northampton NN1 29 E4
Spring Gdns,
Rushden NN10 32 D3
Spring Gdns,
Towcester NN12 38 C4
Spring Gdns,
Wellingborough NN8 40 D4
Spring La, Flore NN7 39 E1
Spring La,
Northampton NN1 28 C3
Spring La*,
The Swansgate Centre
NN8 41 E3
Spring Rise NN15 25 E8
Spring St NN9 22 B4
Spring Ter NN9 22 B4
Springer Straight NN4 28 A6
Springfield NN7 39 E2
Springfield Av NN14 37 D6
Springfield Cl NN15 25 E8
Springfield Gdns MK19 15 A5
Springfield Gro NN17 14 D1
Springfield Rd,
Kettering NN15 25 E8
Springfield Rd,
Peterborough PE8 31 B2
Springfield Rd,
Rushden NN10 33 F7
Springfield Way NN13 12 B2
Springfields NN12 38 A4
Spruce Ct NN16 24 E3
Spur Rd NN8 41 E6
Spurlings PE8 31 B3
Squires Hill NN14 35 B5
Stable Ct NN13 12 C4
Stafford Cl NN11 18 D1
Stamford Rd NN16 24 F4
Standside NN5 28 A4
Stanier Cl NN16 24 C4
Stanion La NN17 14 F2
Stanley Mews NN8 41 F3
Stanley Rd,
Northampton NN5 28 B3
Stanley Rd,
Wellingborough NN8 41 F2
Stanley St,
Kettering NN14 35 C5
Stanley St,
Northampton NN2 28 C2
Stanley Way NN11 18 C2
Stanwell Cl NN17 27 C1
Stanwell Dr OX17 27 C1
Stanwell Lea OX17 27 C1
Stanwell Way NN8 40 B4
Stanwick Rd,
Rushden NN10 32 E1
Stanwick Rd,
Wellingborough NN9 34 A5
Starmers La NN7 21 C4
Station Cl,
Daventry NN11 19 E5
Station Cl,
Long Buckby NN6 23 B5
Station Rd, Corby NN17 14 E2
Station Rd,
Desborough NN14 17 C3
Station Rd,
Earls Barton NN6 20 B3
Station Rd, Finedon NN9 16 A1
Station Rd,
Higham Ferrers NN10 22 D6
Station Rd,
Irthlingborough NN9 22 B4
Station Rd, Isham NN15 13 A3
Station Rd,
Kettering NN15 25 C6
Station Rd,
Long Buckby NN6 23 A6

Station Rd,
Peterborough PE8 31
Station Rd, Rugby CV23 26
Station Rd,
Rushden NN10 33
Station Rd,
Wellingborough NN9 23
Staverton Rd NN11 19
Steane Vw NN13 12
Steel Cl NN14 37
Steele Rd NN8 40
Steene St NN5 29
Stefen Way NN11 19
Stenhouse Cl NN6 23
Stenson Cl NN6 23
Stenson St NN5 28
Stephenson Cl NN11 18
Stephenson Ct,
Northampton NN7 35
Stephenson Ct,
Rugby CV23 26
Stephenson Way NN17 19
Sterndale Cl NN14 17
Stevens Ct NN6 23
Stewart Cl NN3 27
Stewart Dr NN12 36
Stimpson Av NN1 29
Stirling St NN5 29
Stockley St NN1 29
Stocks Hill,
Towcester NN12 38
Stocks Hill,
Wellingborough NN9 16
Stocks Hill*,
Cross St NN3 27
Stoke La NN17 14
Stoke Doyle Rd PE8 31
Stoke Rd NN14 17
Stokes Rd NN18 14
Stone Cl NN29 16
Stratford Rd,
Milton Keynes MK19 15
Stratford Rd,
Northampton NN7 35
Stratton Dr NN13 12
Straws Cl NN9 22
Stream Bank Cl NN8 40
Streatfeild Rd NN5 28
Streather Ct NN9 34
Streather Dr NN17 14
Streeton Way NN6 20
Strode Rd NN8 41
Stronglands Ct PE8 31
Stuart Cl NN16 25
Stuart Rd, Brackley NN13 12
Stuart Rd, Corby NN17 14
Studfall Av NN17 14
Studfall Mews NN17 14
Sturdee Cl NN11 19
Sturton Walk NN18 14
Sulgrave Dr NN17 14
Sulgrave Rd NN5 28
Summerfield Rd NN15 25
Summerlee Rd NN9 16
Sun Hill NN14 35
Sun Yd NN12 38
Sunderland St NN5 28
Sunningdale Dr,
Daventry NN11 18
Sunningdale Dr,
Rushden NN10 33
Sunny Side NN6 20
Surfleet Cl NN18 14
Surrey Cl NN17 14
Surtees Way NN11 18
Sussex Pl NN10 33
Sutherlands Rd NN18 14
Sutton Acre NN7 21
Sutton Bank NN7 35
Sutton Rd PE8 31
Sutton St NN7 35
Swale Cl NN11 18
Swale Dr NN8 40
Swallow Cl NN13 12
Swallow Cl NN14 12
Swallow Dr NN10 33
Swan Cl, Banbury OX17 27
Swan Cl, Brackley NN13 12
Swan Cl,
Burton Latimer NN15 13
Swan Cl,
Thrapston NN14 37
Swan Gdns NN18 14
Swan St NN1 28
Swann Dale NN11 19
Swann Dale D NN10 19
Swans La*,
The Swansgate Centre
NN8 41
Swans Way NN10 33
Swansea Cres NN6 28
Swansea Rd NN5 28
Swanspool Cl NN8 41
Swanspool Par NN8 41
Swift Way NN13 12
Swinburne Cl NN16 24
Swinburne Rd NN8 40
Swinneyford Rd NN12 12
Sycamore Cl,
Daventry NN11 18